MW00532644

Living in the Larger Story

THE CHRISTIAN PSYCHOLOGY OF LARRY CRABB

Jason E. Kanz
Editor

Gideon Institute of Christian
Psychology and Counseling

Copyright © 2019 by Gideon Institute of Christian Psychology and Counseling

All rights reserved. No part of this publication may be reproduced, distributed or transmitted in any form or by any means, including photocopying, recording, or other electronic or mechanical methods, without the prior written permission of the publisher, except in the case of brief quotations embodied in critical reviews and certain other noncommercial uses permitted by copyright law.

Gideon Institute of Christian Psychology and Counseling
Houston Baptist University
7502 Fondren Road
Houston, TX 77074

Scripture quotations marked English Standard Version are Scripture quotations are from The ESV® Bible (The Holy Bible, English Standard Version®), copyright © 2001 by Crossway, a publishing ministry of Good News Publishers. Used by permission. All rights reserved.

Scripture quotations taken from the New American Standard Bible® (NASB), Copyright © 1960, 1962, 1963, 1968, 1971, 1972, 1973, 1975, 1977, 1995 by The Lockman Foundation Used by permission. www.Lockman.org

Scripture taken from the Holy Bible, NEW INTERNATIONAL VERSION®, NIV® Copyright © 1973, 1978, 1984, 2011 by Biblica, Inc.® Used by permission. All rights reserved worldwide.

Scripture quotations marked (NLT) are taken from the Holy Bible, New Living Translation, copyright ©1996, 2004, 2015 by Tyndale House Foundation. Used by permission of Tyndale House Publishers, Inc., Carol Stream, Illinois 60188. All rights reserved.

Cover Photo taken at The Cove in Ashville, NC by Jason E. Kanz

Living in the Larger Story / Jason E. Kanz (ed.) —1st ed.
ISBN 978-0-578-50552-7

For Larry

Friend
Mentor
Teacher
Fellow Pilgrim on the Way

Whatever the cost, make me a little Christ. Father, may your Spirit open the eyes of my heart to see your beauty so that I am left with no greater desire while I live in this world than to reveal your Son's love to others by how I relate.

—Larry Crabb, *A Different Kind of Happiness*

Contents

Acknowledgments

This book would never have happened without the prayers, support, and guidance of many people, some of whom I have never met in person. I am thankful for them all the same.

I am thankful for the chapter authors: Bryan Maier, Dick Averbeck, Bruce Demarest, Colin Dye, Mark McMinn, Gary Moon, Jamie Rasmussen, Siang-Yang Tan, Brett Vaden, Ed Welch, and Kep Crabb. I remain awed at your willingness to be involved in this project. The grace you have each shown to Larry has been granted to me too.

Thank you to Nan Donahoe for your work on the book. Even down to the wire, you were eager to help and were patient with the revisions.

Mark Halvorsen, my dear friend, I cannot imagine working on a project about Larry Crabb without your shared excitement. I miss our monthly radio show, *Crabb Conversations*, but I am glad that we continue to enthusiastically discuss his ideas with one another. Thank you too for your eagerness to offer your suggestions for the book as the deadline loomed large.

Heather, Grace, Ian, and Tessa: What can I say? You love me despite my distracted mind, frequent references to Larry, and marathon writing sessions. I couldn't do any of this without you.

Eric and Larry, you have each influenced me in profound ways. For several years, the two of you have had more influence upon my identity as a Christian psychologist than anyone else. You value my ideas and make me believe I have something to offer. What's more, I am deeply grateful for the friendship I have with each of you. Though you have shaped me professionally, the ways that each of you have cared for me make me a better person.

-Jason Kanz, *Editor*

Contributors

Richard E. Averbeck, Ph.D. is a professor of Old Testament and Semitic studies and the director of the Ph.D. program in theological studies at Trinity Evangelical Divinity School. He has published in a variety of disciplines and is currently committed to several book writing projects including: *The Old Testament Law and the Christian*; *A Rest for the People of God: Reading the Old Testament for the Christian Life*; a commentary on *Leviticus* for the Evangelical Exegetical Commentary series; and a commentary on *Numbers* for the Biblical Theological Christian Proclamation Commentary Series.

Keplen (Kep) Crabb, has been the Executive Director of NewWay Ministries for the past 19 years and is the founder of Larger Story, Inc., a non-profit ministry, created to come alongside spiritually hungry people as they find joy in the midst of heartache, hope even in despair, and faith in the middle of doubt.

Larry Crabb, Ph.D. may be the most influential leader in Christian counseling over the past 50 years. He has written 26 books, including *Inside Out*, *66 Love Letters*, and his most recent, *When God's Ways Make No Sense*, published in 2018. He is a spiritual director, Bible teacher, and popular conference speaker. He is the founder of NewWay Ministries.

Bruce Demarest, Ph.D. is Senior Professor of Christian Theology and Spiritual Formation at Denver Seminary in Littleton, CO. He is the author of multiple books including, *The Cross and Salvation: The Doctrine of Salvation; Seasons of the Soul: Stages of Spiritual Development;* and *Satisfy Your Heart: Restoring the Heart of Christian Spirituality.*

Colin Dye, B.Div. is the Senior Leader of the Kensington Temple, London City Church and founder of the International Bible Institute of London. He has been involved in pastoral ministry for the past 40 years. He is the author of 40 books including the 12 volume *Sword of the Spirit* materials available in seven languages.

Eric L. Johnson, Ph.D. is Professor of Christian Psychology at Houston Baptist University. He has published over 50 articles and three books: *Foundations for Soul Care: A Christian Psychology Proposal; Psychology and Christianity: Five Fiews* (editor); and *God and Soul Care: The Therapeutic Resources of the Christian Faith.* He is the founding director of the Society for Christian Psychology and of the Gideon Institute for Christian Psychology and Counseling.

Jason E. Kanz, Ph.D. is a board certified neuropsychologist in clinical practice at the Marshfield Clinic in Eau Claire, Wisconsin. He has authored or co-authored several scientific and professional articles on topics ranging from neuropsychology and neuroimaging to forgiveness and clinical supervision. He also published a book of poetry based upon the Psalms, *Soil of the Divine.*

Bryan N. Maier, Psy.D. is a recently appointed professor of Counseling at Cairn University having previously served for many years in various clinical and academic positions. He is the author of *Forgiveness and Justice: A Christian Approach.*

Mark R. McMinn, Ph.D. is Professor of Psychology and Director of Faith Integration in the Graduate Department of Clinical Psychology at George Fox University and a licensed psychologist in Oregon. Mark is board certified in clinical psychology by the American Board of Professional Psychology. The author of more than a dozen books, his most recent book is *The Science of Virtue: Why Positive Psychology Matters to the Church.*

Gary W. Moon, Ph.D. has been a licensed psychologist for 30 years. He is the founding Executive Director of the Martin Institute for Christianity and Culture and the Dallas Willard Center for Christian Spiritual Formation at Westmont College from 2011 to 2018, and continues in leadership. He served as the founding director of the Renovaré International Institute for Christian Spiritual Formation; and as a founding co-editor of the *Conversations Journal* (together with Larry Crabb and David Benner), and is the author of several books, including a recent biography of Dallas Willard, *Becoming Dallas Willard: The Formation of a Philosopher, Teacher, and Christ Follower.*

Jamie Rasmussen, M.Div. has served as the Senior Pastor of Scottsdale Bible Church since 2007, reaching more than 6,000 people each week and an estimated 15,000 people each month with his transformational messages. He recently published *How Joyful People Think.*

Siang-Yang Tan, Ph.D. is Professor of Psychology at Fuller Theological Seminary in Pasadena, California and Senior Pastor of First Evangelical Church Glendale. He is a licensed psychologist and Fellow of the American Psychological Association. He has published numerous articles and books, including *Counseling and Psychotherapy: A Christian Perspective* and *Shepherding God's People: A Guide to Faithful and Fruitful Pastoral Ministry.*

Brett Vaden, M.Div., Ph.D. is the Academic Dean of the Three Fourteen Institute and the Director of Discipleship and Curriculum Development at The Journey church in St. Louis. His research interests focus on authenticity, the true self and false self, the writings of Thomas Merton, and the works of C. S. Lewis and J. R. R. Tolkien.

Ed Welch, M.Div., Ph.D. is a counselor and faculty member at the Christian Counseling and Education Foundation. He is a leader in the biblical counseling movement, speaks around the world, and has written over a dozen books including *When People are Big and God is Small; Shame, Interrupted;* and *Caring for One*

Another: 8 Ways to Cultivate Meaningful Relationships.

Forward

Narratives pervade all complex cultures, including their religions and life-philosophies, but they are especially important in theistic cultures, since theism—the view that a personal God and God's creation are fundamentally different orders of being—assumes movement between the infinite God and finite humans. According to theism, humans are either moving toward God, ascending ever closer to him through their religious activities (as assumed in non-Christian theisms), or God is moving toward sinful humans, descending to his fallen creatures—most spectacularly in the incarnation of the Son of God—and redeeming them from their fallen predicament (as assumed in Christian theism). Monism—the view that all reality is one—by contrast, has no need of movement. Humans already possess all that they need; they only have to become awakened and realize what they possess.

We see how important narratives are in the Bible, where a grand metanarrative is revealed, the "larger story" within which we are to understand human life, and much of the content of Scripture consists of narratives of patriarchs, kings, prophets, and apostles, organized around the four gospel accounts of the story of Jesus Christ and communicating the triune God's movement toward humanity and humanity's response. On a personal level, the stories of Christians are each a narrative of movement too, of God coming to seek and to save the lost (Luke 19:10), raising them from the dead (Luke 15:32; Ephesians 2:6), more and more, as they personally appropriate his grace, in a narrative journey that takes as long as they live, which according to Edwards (1852/1969, Ch. 16), may continue on forever.

Larry Crabb is a Christian whose story has impacted many lives over the past few decades, including mine. Part of that influence was his authorship of many books during this time period, and this series of written works allows readers to trace the arc of his own story of divinely-bestowed maturation and participation, and discern something of the progress of God's working in his mind and heart and character (not unlike the progress of grace evident in Augustine's writings). The opening chapter of this book charts his journey and enables people to see a growing saint becoming more balanced, deeper, and increasingly Christ-centered and Spirit-shaped over the course of his life. I'll let the authors of that chapter tell the story, but I point to it, because it illustrates God's intention for all of his people, both individually and corporately, to respond to God's movement towards us, by drawing nearer to God (James 4:8), and becoming more and more conformed to the image of Christ (Romans 8:29). Larry also frequently draws upon the image of dancing; surely God's movement toward us and our response also constitutes a kind of dance.

There are thousands of corporate ways that God's movement, and our own, has happened in the history of the church and is happening among Christians in our day. One of those ways is the story of Christian psychology.

The church has been developing a psychology for millennia. Beginning with the inspired lay psychology of the Bible, composed of various genres that uniquely offer essential psychologically-relevant themes, particularly focused on humanity's redemption in Christ, yet absent the genre of a systematic body of psychological knowledge. As a result, others took up the seminal insights of the Bible and developed them further, building on one another intertextually, such as Augustine, Bernard of Clairvaux, Aquinas, Julian of Norwich, Calvin, Luther, Edwards, Pascal, and Kierkegaard (1849/1980), who might be considered the father of Christian psychology, since he referred to himself as a Christian psychologist and subtitled one of his most important books, *The Sickness Unto Death*, "A Christian Psychological Exposition for Upbuilding and Awakening." Yes, Kierkegaard thought Christians needed to be "woke," but it was an awakening that primarily involved loving God supremely and seeing him as the center of reality and, secondarily, loving one's neighbor as oneself, which is the inevitable, human-relational implication of the logically-prior ultimate reorientation (Matthew 22:37-38).

Like many Christians, Kierkegaard was further along intellectually than he was relationally or virtuously, which partly explains why he had no disciples (contrary to Freud; see Garff, 2013, for Kierkegaard's story, and Jones, 1953-57, for Freud's). As a result, his insights laid largely dormant for decades, while the church was in a period of gradual stagnation and declension. In the meantime, a secular revolution was occurring (Smith, 2003) that coincided with the flourishing of a secular psychology, aided by the application of the methods of the natural sciences to the study of human phenomena.

Larry Crabb was educated long after this secular revolution had occurred. By the time he came of age, Christians had to get a Ph.D. in secular psychology, if they wanted to work in psychotherapy and counseling. In his (1975, 1977) earliest writings, Crabb sought to describe a distinctly Christian alternative, which nonetheless borrowed from secular psychology without apology. Though titled "biblical counseling," they were actually among the best examples of the integration approach to psychotherapy and counseling then emerging. Beginning with *Understanding People* (1987) and *Inside Out* (1988), however, his work became increasingly marked by the teachings of Scripture and a God-centeredness uncommon among integrationists, and later, a familiarity with some of the pre-modern psychologists and caregivers of the Christian tradition. He eventually aligned his journey with the teachings and practices of classic Christian spirituality, combining a clinical sensibility with a devotional orientation that promoted self-awareness, authenticity, ethical responsibility towards others, and a deepening relationship with God.

Concurrent with the first shift in Crabb's writings was a fresh call to the project of a Christian psychology by the Christian philosophers Robert Roberts (1988) and C. Stephen Evans (1989; 1990) who challenged Christians in the field of psychology to look to philosophy for inspiration, pointing to the example of Kierkegaard, as well as the contemporary renewal of distinctively Christian philosophy that was then in ascendency. IGNIS: The Institute for Christian Psychology had recently been founded (in 1986), and by 1989 their five staff members were practicing distinctly Christian therapy, holding conferences and symposia, teaching courses in Christian psychology, and publishing the IGNIS-Journal, and had initiated a three-year training course in Christian therapy. Throughout the 90s, non-professional forms of Christian soul care continued to spread among laypeople and ministers, for example, biblical counseling, healing prayer, and Christian spirituality, and other popular-level texts reflecting a Christian psychology orientation were being written by David Benner, Siang-Yang Tan, Diane Langberg, Dan Allender & Tremper Longman III, and Sandra Wilson, among others. Early in the 21st century, the Institute of Spiritual Formation was established at Biola University, with John Coe as director; the Society for Christian Psychology was founded in the United States in 2003, becoming a division of the American Association of Christian Counselors in 2005 (Larry Crabb was a speaker at a Society conference in 2007); and the European Movement of Christian Anthropology, Psychology, and Psychotherapy was holding conferences (see Joubert, 2019, for a collection of conference papers) and later published an online magazine, *Christian Psychology Around the World* (May, 2012-2019).

One of the greatest needs of the Christian psychology movement in North America has been the lack of corresponding graduate education that leads to licensure. The Gideon Institute of Christian Psychology and Counseling was established in 2019 to address that need, as well as to hold conferences and develop a counseling center for the students of Houston Baptist University and the surrounding community, and eventually to do distinctly Christian psychological research and theory-building. In light of the overlapping stories summarized above, it is fitting that the first book published by the Gideon Institute (and its first conference) is a celebration of the contributions of Larry Crabb to Christian counseling and to the people of God.

Which brings us to the theme alluded to in the title of the book: *Living in the Larger Story*. As suggested above, human history is best understood as a story originating in the Trinity, which mysteriously invites our conscious, dependent participation. We would like to suggest that Larry Crabb's life and works are a notable part of the story of Christian psychology of the last 30 years; and the Christian psychology movement, such as it is, is a subplot of the larger story that provides the transcendent context for every human being: the temporal revelation of the triune God's glory, particularly through his people, images of God who take up his invitation to live our lives within *the* image of God, Jesus Christ, collaborating with him in the manifestation of the Father's glory, just as he prayed, "The glory that you have given me, I have given to them, that they may be one even as we are one, I in them and you in me, that they may become perfectly one, so that the world may know that you sent me and loved them even as you loved me." (John 17:22-23, English Standard Version) Ultimately, *that*, is what this book is about.

Eric L. Johnson, Ph.D., *Director of the Gideon Institute*

Introduction

Now in his 70s, Larry Crabb has been practicing Christian Psychology for longer than I have been alive. He published his first book in 1975 and since then, has been a prodigious author. He has published more than two dozen books that most people would describe as representing "Christian psychology;" however, I believe you will discover as you read through this book that his thinking has evolved over the decades into a fuller, richer understanding of soul care. His is not a sterile, academic psychology, but one that is born out of a life spent wrestling with God, living through periods of great blessing, great doubt, and great suffering, themes explored with an almost uncomfortable clarity in his recent book, *When God's Ways Makes No Sense* (2018).

In this book, we explore the development of Crabb's thinking in his published works, identifying the trajectory of his thinking as well as highlighting themes that seem to recur in his writings. Several respondents, representing various backgrounds, contributed short chapters including: Richard Averbeck, Kep Crabb, Bruce Demarest, Colin Dye, Mark McMinn, Gary Moon, Jamie Rasmussen, Brett Vaden, Ed Welch, and Siang Yang Tan. Dr. Crabb himself graciously wrote an extended reflection as the concluding piece.

On a personal level, few people have had such a significant effect upon the way I think about the Christian life as Larry has had. I have been fortunate to attend his School for Spiritual Direction, which had a profound impact upon me personally and professionally.

I have been mentored by his books and instruction, but above all, I am grateful for a friend who has faithfully shown me what life looks like on the road less traveled.

Jason Kanz, Ph.D., *Editor*

JASON E. KANZ & BRYAN N. MAIER

THE CHRISTIAN PSYCHOLOGY OF LARRY CRABB: A CAREER ON THE ROAD LESS TRAVELED

I n this essay, it is our goal to present an overview of the life and writings of Larry Crabb as an exemplar of Christian psychology. We are fortunate to have access to four decades of his writings, which reveal a continued commitment to Christian psychology. Each of us has benefited from personal exposure to Dr. Crabb and undoubtedly, our individual experiences color this essay. Finally, Dr. Crabb kindly provided background information to the first author in support of this article.

In the preface to *Foundations of Soul Care* (2007), Johnson wrote: "The project of a Christian psychology is not yet widely understood, and there will always be different notions of just what it is. Most of its proponents, however, I think would agree that it aims at the development of a distinctly Christian *version* of psychology: a wise science of individual human beings that includes theory building, research, teaching, training, and various kinds of practice, including the care of souls. This science flows from a Christian understanding of human nature and therefore can be distinguished from alternative versions of psychology based on different world views" (p. 9). As we review Dr. Crabb's professional work, we hope it is evident that he has approached each of these aims for several decades to a degree where it is reasonable to assert that there is a distinctly "Crabbian" approach to soul care that captures the heart of Johnson's proposal.

We hope to demonstrate that Dr. Crabb is a prototypical example of what Christian psychologists may aspire to achieve and extend. We will begin by providing a biographical sketch of Dr. Crabb. We will then proceed to provide a chronological overview of his published works. After cataloging his works, we will discuss common themes beneficial to understand his ideas.

Brief Biographical Sketch[1]

Larry Crabb Jr. was born in 1944 in Evanston, Illinois, the second son born to Lawrence and Isabel Crabb. In 1946, the family moved to Philadelphia, Pennsylvania where his father owned and operated the

---

[1] Although some details regarding this biographical sketch were gleaned from his extant writings, the general framework and details were provided to Dr. Kanz in September 2015. Thank you to Dr. Crabb for his willingness to share this overview of his life.

Power Tool Company. Larry had a religious upbringing, his family faithfully attending the Plymouth Brethren church.

He performed well in school, particularly in English classes. When he was in the fifth grade, his teacher stopped him and said, "Larry, you seem to like words. Someday, you'll write a book." At the encouragement of that teacher, he began to work on his first "book effort" for 30 minutes each day. Something about those words was life-giving to Crabb, and he remembers feeling a "curious excitement" (Crabb, 2015).

In 1961, after completing high school, he enrolled in Ursinus College. Although he initially explored journalism and physical education, by the middle of his sophomore year, he settled upon a psychology major, noting that he believed "hypnosis would be interesting" (Crabb, 2015).

After graduating from Ursinus, he began doctoral studies in clinical psychology at the University of Illinois, a program consistently ranked in the top five nationally. He again performed well academically, graduating first in his Ph.D. class in 1970. While working on his doctoral studies, his writing was again recognized. A professor for whom he had considerable respect held up one of his papers during class as the finest paper he had ever read. In the final year of his doctoral studies, on a dare, he submitted an article "Data and Dogma as Compatible" to *Christianity Today* (1971). The magazine published the article, and it became Crabb's first paid writing assignment also opening the door to the Christian publishing world (Crabb, 2015).

Upon graduation, he became the director of counseling services at Florida Atlantic University, a position he held for two years. The time at FAU "provided opportunity to think through and compare psychological solutions to the human dilemma with biblical answers to life's questions." (Crabb, 2015). He left that position and, with the support of his friends and family, began to explore Christian Psychology in greater depth while starting a private practice in Florida. He fortuitously was introduced to the founder of Zondervan Publishing, which led to the publishing of his first book, *Basic Principles of Biblical Counseling* (Crabb, 1975).

As he continued in his private practice, he became increasingly convinced that "what professionals called 'psychotherapy' could better be understood as passionate, wisdom-based conversations" (Crabb, 2015), an understanding that has persisted in his writing and thinking. He left his private practice to develop a master's degree program at Grace Theological Seminary in Indiana where his colleagues, Dan Allender and Tom Varney, helped further his thinking. As he continued to develop and disseminate his ideas, he came under increased scrutiny, accused of "psychoheresy" and "dragging Freud into the Scriptures." In the face of these criticisms, he was dismissed from Grace in the late 1980s and transferred to the master's program at Colorado Christian University in 1990 (Crabb, 2015).

Around the turn of the century, he was increasingly drawn to the idea of spiritual formation and started

NewWay Ministries, where he continues today. Through NewWay Ministries, Dr. Crabb has continued his writing ministry, having recently completed his 26th book, *When God's Ways Make No Sense* (Crabb, 2018). He has also remained committed to sharing his ideas about soul care through week-long intensives, which he has called "schools for spiritual direction," or SSDs, which have surpassed 70 in number.

In addition to his professional development, Dr. Crabb would readily acknowledge that his personal story has affected his career trajectory. He married Rachael, his childhood sweetheart, in 1966 after his first year at the University of Illinois. They recently celebrated 50 years of marriage. They have two sons, Kep and Ken. He has spoken publicly about the effect of the loss of his parents, his mother to Alzheimer's disease. He also lost his older brother Bill in a plane crash outside of Colorado Springs in 1991. A long battle with cancer, including the development of a second type of cancer, leukemia, in 2018, has influenced his thinking about soul care and his sense of urgency to continue in ministry, even into his mid-70s. Thus far, he shows no signs of a quiet retirement.

Dr. Crabb has been shaped by over 7 decades of professional and personal life. His life has been replete with joys and sorrows. In many ways, his approach to soul care and his own ideas of what constitutes a Christian Psychology have been shaped and morphed not only by his professional knowledge, but also by his individual and relational journey. As we move into exploring the content of his writing, you will begin to see a deepening model of soul care shaped by a life well lived.

Annotated Bibliography

In the late 1970s and early 1980s, there were two broad schools of thought regarding what constituted biblical soul care. For many people, engaging a Christian psychology involved little more than identifying as a Christian. Adherents of the levels-of-explanation approach understood that being a Christian should make a difference in how people think and act, but unless psychological theories involved blatant contradictions with their faith, this group viewed themselves similarly to Christian doctors or plumbers— there is no distinctly Christian way to remove a gall bladder or unplug a drain (although there might be prayers in both cases), but the doctor or the plumber can perform his task in a skilled and professional manner and give God the glory for any and all successes. Integrationists worked hard to consolidate psychology and Christian thought, yet psychology continued to provide the primary framework. Thus being an excellent and ethical professional constituted being biblical for some psychologists.

Though their approaches to "Christian psychology" were in many regards quite distinct from one another, the integrationists and levels-of-explanation groups probably represented the majority of Christian counselors at that time, yet there was a significant minority of thinkers for whom these approaches were not sufficiently "biblical." They believed that because sin was the cause of mental health problems, the solutions were located squarely and exclusively within Scripture itself. If the problem could be found in scripture, so could the solution. Biblical counselors who invoked secular thinkers like Freud, Skinner, and Rogers were in error. Proponents of this view, principally Jay Adams (nouthetic counseling), attempted to construct a model of biblical counseling that was thoroughly and solely biblical[2].

Basic Principles of Biblical Counseling (1975)

Around the time that the integrationists, levels of explanation proponents, and nouthetic counselors were attempting to understand what being biblical meant, Dr. Crabb also entered the discussion with the publication of *Basic Principles of Biblical Counseling* (1975). In the introduction to the book, Crabb acknowledged that "it became clearly and frighteningly apparent that most of what [he] was believing and doing as a professional psychologist was built upon the swaying foundation of humanism" (Crabb, 1975, p. 11). He entered the project desiring to understand and explain a truly biblical model of counseling. Disillusioned with existing models, he sought to develop "a substantial understanding of the problem of people and of the best ways to deal with

---

[2] For additional discussion of the history and description of the various understandings of Psychology and Christianity, please consult *Psychology and Christianity: Five Views* (Johnson & Myers, 2010).

them which could *rightfully* claim to be thoroughly biblical" (italics ours, Crabb, 1975, p. 12).

Drawing upon the influence of Francis Schaeffer, Crabb explored the bankruptcy of humanistic optimism and existing models of psychotherapy, though he was careful to acknowledge that he did not want to "cavalierly dismiss secular psychotherapy" (Crabb, 1975, p. 26). He presented a respectful critique and rebuttal of the popular secular theories including Freudianism, ego psychology, Rogerian approaches, Existentialism, and secular behaviorism.

As he moved from sharing these critiques to providing his own understanding, he presented a model that appears to have been influenced by cognitive-type therapies. On page 46, he wrote, "I believe that a failure to identify and correct *wrong thinking* is responsible for much of the repeated failure of people who sincerely try to live the Christian life" (italics ours, Crabb, 1975). He was critical of Carl Rogers, noting he "took us ten steps backward by minimizing what a person thinks and focusing on feelings" (p. 77, Crabb, 1975). In the seventh chapter of the book, he strongly argued for the necessity of confronting faulty thinking.

However, as he continued to develop his early thinking, he did not simply stop at a Christianized version of cognitive behavioral therapy (CBT). Beginning in chapter 5, he explored issues outside of disrupted thinking. He noted that the results of sin involved separation from God, separation from others, separation from nature, and separation from self (Crabb, 1975, p. 49). Although in some regards his focus on sin was complementary to biblical counselor Jay Adams, he pushed deeper. He wrote, "There is more to real counseling than rebuke and exhortation. Teaching a new way of thinking, correcting wrong ways of thinking which underlie wrong behavior and feelings is central" (p. 50).

He also began to foreshadow some of his later thinking. In addition to addressing disrupted thinking, he described the importance of relationship, primarily with God and secondarily with others. "He has designed the loving fellowship of believers to be the visible means of demonstrating his love to each other and to the world" (Crabb, 1975, p. 74). His relational thinking was perhaps in its infancy in *Basic Principles of Biblical Counseling*, but it was assuredly there.

Effective Biblical Counseling (1977)

In his sophomore offering, his stated goal was to "offer the philosophical and conceptual thinking upon which [he builds his] counseling approach" (p. 13). Themes of relationship and right thinking continued to find their way into this book, but were developed more fully than they were in *Basic Principles of Biblical Counseling* (Crabb, 1975). Crabb viewed the primary goal of the Christian life as growth in maturity, which involves "two elements: 1) immediate obedience in specific situations and 2) long-range character growth" (Crabb, 1977, p. 23). Therefore, a key to understanding Crabb's thinking at the time was that: "Christian counseling is concerned with whether or not the client is responding obediently to whatever circumstances he is experiencing" (p.25). Obedience and behavior change are accomplished primarily by challenging one's thinking.

Crabb (2015) indicated that a primary motivation in writing *Effective Biblical Counseling* (1977) was that he was "determined to understand a biblical theology of how change occurs." He viewed Romans 12:1-2 as consistent with Aaron Beck's Cognitive Therapy, so attention to the thought life remained a primary focus. Yet as he explored the personality structure, he wrote about not only conscious thinking, but the unconscious mind, a person's basic direction (heart), the capacity for choice (will), and feeling or emotion.

In *Basic Principles of Biblical Counseling* (1975), Crabb began to critique the various psychological models. In *Effective Biblical Counseling* (Crabb, 1977), he provided a critique of existing approaches to Christian soul care. He described the various attempts as "separate but equal," "tossed salad," and "nothing buttery," which may in turn represent: levels-of-explanation, integration, and traditional biblical counseling approaches. In response, he proposed a fourth attempt: "spoiling the Egyptians." He proposed that "anyone who wants to work toward a truly evangelical integration of Christianity and psychology should meet the following qualifications": 1) psychology must be under the authority of Scripture, 2) fervent insistence that the Bible is God's infallible, inspired, inerrant revelation, 3) Scripture must have functional control over thinking (biblical priority), and 4) a serious interest in and a general grasp of Scripture (p. 49-50).

Crabb was issuing a call for a distinctly Christian psychology in 1977. Near the end of the book, Crabb proposed a simple model for counseling (p. 146ff). His proposed stages were as follows:

1. Identify problem feelings
2. Identify goal-oriented (problem) behavior
3. Identify problem thinking
4. Change the assumptions/clarify biblical thinking
5. Secure commitment
6. Plan and carry out biblical behavior
7. Identify Spirit-controlled feelings

Despite hints of a broader theory of counseling and personality, *Effective Biblical Counseling* (1977) continued to present a largely cognitive behavioral approach to change.

The Adventures of Captain Al Scabbard (1981)

This two book set is a striking departure from the rest of Crabb's writings, which focus on issues broadly connected with soul care and Christian psychology. Crabb created the fictional crime fighter, Al Scabbard, in order to help instruct his two young sons. He commented, "C.S. Lewis caught me with his thought that a child learns more from what a hero of the child assumes than from what a culturally assigned teacher teaches. I therefore created a hero to compete with such TV heroes as Incredible Hulk who never taught against God; he just never mentioned Him. Scabbard never taught Christianity, but he obviously assumed its truth" (Crabb, 2015).

The Marriage Builder (1982/1992/2013)[3]

The Marriage Builder (1982) was written after perceiving that the flame in his marriage to Rachael had died (Crabb, 2015). He presented marriage, perhaps that most complex of human relationships, as ultimately other-centered, relational, and involving a leap of faith. The idea that marriage is other-centered has been present in most Christian marriage books for many years, standing in contrast to what would become known as the "me generation." During the time of its writing in the 1980s, scriptures such as Mark 12:28-31, outlining the two great commandments (love God and love your neighbor), were being turned upside down to say one could not fulfill either of these two great mandates until one fulfills an unspoken, prerequisite commandment to love oneself. Bringing a self-centered attitude into marriage did not require much of a change in priorities. Crabb resisted cultural trends and spoke again of the marital call to love one's spouse (and by doing so to love one's God). In the preface to the 2013 edition, he wrote, "fulfilling personal needs is the ultimate value, even among far too many Christians,"[4] but "marriage presents a unique opportunity to put the gospel of Jesus Christ into place" (Crabb, 1982, p. 7).

---

[3] A condensed version of *Marriage Builder* was released in 1998 under the title of *How to Become One with Your Mate*.

[4] Quotations are taken from the 2013 edition.

THE CHRISTIAN PSYCHOLOGY OF LARRY CRABB • 33

Crabb recognized the risk of exploitation or
unrequited love, yet encouraged spouses to take the risk
anyway because of the safety net of God's love. Crabb's
understanding of human flourishing was developing at
this point. He noted that one's deepest need is not a
loving spouse, but a restored relationship with God, a
theme that would come to form much of his later
ministry. If spouses prioritize loving God well, they are
positioned to love their spouses sacrificially. He
expressed concern in the belief that happiness and
fulfillment, rather than holiness, have been prioritized in
marriage (Crabb, 1982, p. 13).

Early in the book, Crabb explored the role of needs,
suggesting that every person has two principle needs:
love and meaning. We are not simply automatons or
complex machines; we possess legitimate needs as those
created in God's image (Crabb, 1982, p. 39ff). In the
chapter entitled "Spirit Oneness," he presented four
different approaches to dealing with our needs: 1)
ignoring them, 2) looking for satisfaction in
achievement, 3) attempting to meet our needs in one
another, or 4) depending upon the Lord to meet them.
He cautioned against the first three, but his counsel
under the third point is particularly poignant. Though it
makes some intuitive sense to seek our ultimate
satisfaction in our marriage relationship, he warned that
this approach could be exploitative. He wryly identified
the problems inherent in a "tick on a dog" relationship,
where this type of marriage has two ticks and no dog, or
two takers, a clear image that reveals Crabb's ability to
use humor to succinctly describe more complex

thinking. Unsurprisingly, reliance upon the Lord is viewed as ideal. "Husbands and wives are to regard marriage as an opportunity to minister in a unique and special way to another human being, to be used of God to bring their spouses into a more satisfying appreciation of their worth as persons who are secure and significant in Jesus Christ" (Crabb, 1982, p. 72).

Evidences of Cognitive-Behavioral Therapy continued to show their influence in *The Marriage Builder* (1982). For example, when describing a counseling relationship with a married woman, he noted how, after conflict, she "played a tape" confirming her husband's rejection of her and how he prepared a new tape for her to repeat to herself to remind her of her value in God (Crabb, 1982, p. 51-52).

Encouragement (1984/2013)

Co-written with Dan Allender, *Encouragement: The Unexpected Power of Building Others Up* (Crabb & Allender, 1984) went still deeper into exploring the importance of relationship. One of the verses that has formed much of Crabb's writing and thinking was foundational to this book. Hebrews 10:24-25 (New International Version) reads, "Consider how we may spur one another on to love and good deeds, not giving up meeting together...but *encouraging* one another— and all the more as you see the Day approaching." With an ongoing commitment to understanding soul care from a biblical perspective, Crabb and Allender sought to understand biblical encouragement. For the authors, the biblical way to address human hurts was through relationship, with God and in community.

Drawing also from Proverbs 18:21, they described how words may bring death and life. Too often, faith communities live on the surface of life, failing to move below the depths of one another's lives. When we do speak, our words may harm, but they may also give life. On page 26, Crabb shared a story from childhood that was deeply formative. As a stutterer praying at the Lord's Supper as a young man, he felt embarrassed. However, at the close of service, one of the older men in the church stopped him and said, "Larry, there's one thing I want you to know. Whatever you do for the Lord, I am behind you one thousand percent."[5] That one sentence was life giving.

Although a commitment to other-centeredness seemed to emerge in *The Marriage Builder* (Crabb, 1982), it took on greater depth in *Encouragement* (1984). Crabb, together with Allender, wrote meaningfully about the biblical call to build others up.

Hope When You're Hurting (1985)

In *Hope When You're Hurting* (1985), Crabb and Allender sought to answer "four questions hurting people ask": 1) What's wrong? 2) Who can help? 3) What will the helper do? and 4) What can I hope for?

At the outset, Crabb restated his belief that counseling can and should happen at the *local* level, more so than in professional counseling offices. He

---

[5] Quotations are taken from the 2013 edition.

wrote, "Part of our problem is our assumption that real help for real problems requires the services of an expert" (Crabb & Allender, 1985, p. 58). Crabb, however, has been stalwart in his desire to train people at a local level to care for hurting people.

He also discussed the importance of connection, an idea that began to describe one of his primary ministry aims. He wrote, "Connection, not analysis, seems closer to the center of my work," perhaps foreshadowing his 1997 book, *Connecting*. Unfortunately, much of modern psychology seeks first to explain the human condition rather than to relate to others well. This need for explanation is seen in what Crabb later would call "the managed life," though he began to hint at that in this book.

The importance of the Trinity is foundational to Crabb's current thinking. Although he explores Trinitarian theology more deeply in later books, he began that exploration here. Discussing perichoresis, he wrote, "When God created us in His image, He intended that we would similarly pour into one another from the deepest resources of our being. When this pouring takes place, there is connection. Disconnection, I suggest, lies behind most of the problems we take to counselors" (Crabb & Allender, 1985, p. 170). Those familiar with Crabb's current thinking will recognize the importance of these ideas in this relatively early book.

Understanding People (1987/2013)[6]

In *Understanding People: Deep Longings for Relationship* (1987), Crabb proposed a model for understanding human psychological functioning, with the hope that it would allow increased dialog between the various groups identifying with biblical counseling, acknowledging a long history of difference and animosity between those aligning with different perspectives.

Before presenting his model, Crabb reasserted an assumption that has guided his personal and professional life. In Part 1 of the book, he addressed the importance of biblical authority. He stated concisely: "counseling models must demonstrate more than mere consistency with Scripture; they must in fact emerge from it"[7] (Crabb, 1987, p. 31). Crabb has often had to fend off attacks from multiple critics; psychologists criticizing him as not paying sufficient attention to the existing psychological literature, and conservative biblicists claiming that he was not only not biblical, but frankly heretical. Despite these criticisms, Crabb restated his desire to be truly biblical. "As I seek to develop a model of counseling, I begin with the conviction that my study of God's written Word must be allowed to control my thinking more than any other data. Where the Bible speaks, it speaks with authority. Where it doesn't speak, we may look to other sources of information for help" (p. 48).

After his analysis of secular theories in his earlier books, and a reassurance of his commitment to biblical authority, the next logical step was for Crabb to map out

---

[6] *Understanding People* was also released in a condensed, gift-book version in 1992 under the title *Understanding Who You Are*.

[7] Quotations are taken from the 2013 edition.

his own model of psychological functioning. His starting point was this: "People are fallen image bearers" (Crabb, 1987, p. 97). The duality of human value and human brokenness thus figured prominently in how he proceeded in developing his model.

His emerging model consisted of four concentric circles, implying dependence or a hierarchy of the different aspects of inner nature of human beings. The idea that how one thinks (Circle #2—rational) influences behavior (Circle #3—volitional) and emotions (Circle #4—emotional) was consistent with cognitive behaviorism, which as we have already noted, shaped some of Crabb's earlier thinking and predominated secular psychotherapy at the time. But now Crabb added something new. He believed that the Bible demonstrated that deep longings (Circle #1—personal) had even greater influence than the rational circle. With this broadened understanding, he came to believe that seeking to understand unconscious motivations and drives also played a significant role in developing a more comprehensive understanding of people. Love and affections reside in Circle #1. The personal circle is where the longing for connection with God and others was found. So affections, not cognition, were predominant. This was a rather novel idea at a time when cognitive behavioral and rational emotive therapies were the prevailing paradigms. Simply, Crabb noted that each of us is: "a personal being who longs deeply, a rational being who thinks, a volitional being who chooses, and an emotional being who feels" (Crabb, 1987, p. 106). As we grapple with each of these aspects, ideally in loving community, we move toward maturity, which is "most clearly visible in the way people relate to one another" (p. 218).

Inside Out (1988/2007/2013)

With additional shifts in thinking, *Inside Out* (1988) became Crabb's best-selling book. His earlier writings, even through *Understanding People* (Crabb, 1987), were often built upon a cognitive-behavioral skeleton. *Inside Out* was different from, or at least more explicit than, all of his previous writings in exploring unmet desires for heaven, tendencies toward self-protection, and accompanying relational sin.

In *Inside Out* (1988), Crabb began to develop the idea that there is something that motivates people beyond the rational, perhaps initially explored in the "personal circle" described in *Understanding People* (1987). People frequently act contrary to their rational assessment of what should be done in specific situations. It is at this point that Crabb makes an Augustinian turn by exploring the biblical concept of *thirst*. Thirst is not merely the result of mental, or cognitive, processes, it is a basic longing. At the level of our souls, there exists within each person a created longing that cannot be satisfied by anything other than God. The biblical metaphor for this longing is thirst (Matthew 5:6, John 6:35). Because we are derivative of a Trinitarian God (i.e., made in His image), we were not created to be independent; rather, we are made to be primarily dependent on our Creator.

Our essential need for God is why thirst is never condemned in Scripture. Instead, it is assumed. Too often, we conclude that if we just did not want something so badly; if we could just "control our baser desires" or "put to death the flesh," we would be able to live according to the wisdom and principles that our rational minds have gleaned from sermons and Bible study. Rather than condemn us for being thirsty, the Bible judges us based on where we go to quench our thirst. Why do "broken cisterns" (Jeremiah 2:13) seem to satisfy?

The concept of thirst leads to a second and related theme of *Inside Out* (1988). Crabb suggested that it is not deep, created longings that cause problems, but rather the wrong strategies people employ to meet those deep created longings. At the time *Inside Out* was written, this was almost a complete reversal of the standard Christian approach to dealing with personal problems. The common wisdom then (and even to some degree now) is that if we could just purge ourselves of our deep desires we would not be taken captive by their malignant power. It is hard to become an addict if you have domesticated every desire. Of course, the logical outgrowth of this position is that Christians who adopt it (even subconsciously) are functioning more as Buddhists than believers in the God of the Bible. The growing influences of Augustine, C.S. Lewis (1949), and John Piper (1986) were seen in *Inside Out*. Rather than trying to suppress desire and longings, Crabb challenged his readers to pursue and celebrate *right* desires (especially desire for God), arguing that our thirst is what makes them truly human. The problem then is not that we desire too much but rather that we desire too little.

As he considered motivation, thirst, and longing, he invited his readers to inner work and not merely behavioral change. Most Christians, he suggested, are what might be called "shallow copers", individuals who have become relatively adept at denying their deep thirst, yet miss the core of who they are. The other group consists of "troubled reflectors," those who "know something is terribly wrong and, as a result, struggle in their efforts to move along through life"[8] (Crabb, 1988, p. 51).

Unfortunately, our fallen nature often results in sinful strategies to quench thirst. Drawing from Jeremiah 2:13, Crabb suggested that people often pursue ineffective means to meet real needs and so lasting change does not happen. People may seek fulfilment in sinful activities (e.g., consuming pornography), amoral activities (e.g., exercise), or even things they were created to be involved with, such as human relationship. However, when casual longings, critical longings, and crucial longings are confused (Crabb, 1988, p. 101), thirst remains unquenched. *Inside Out* helps the reader to grow in understanding deep longings and move toward others in love.

---

[8] Quotations are taken from the 2013 edition.

Men and Women (1991/2013)

Crabb (2015) described *Men and Women: Enjoying the Difference* (1991) as "essentially a follow-up to *Inside Out*," examining how self-protection, explored in the former book, plays out in relationships between men and women. The first half of *Men and Women* is broadly applicable, even beyond gender roles as the title would suggest. As has often been true of Crabb, he did not follow paths previously trodden by those trying to understand biblical counseling, but struck out on his own in a third direction, trying to reclaim a true Christian psychology. He wrote,

"In Christian circles, two popular approaches to building relationships exist. Though they are different, each moves us away from correcting our deep problem of self-centeredness. The first approach insists that suffering is such an unthinkable violation of a person's dignity that nothing matters more than healing wounds and restoring identity...The second approach clubs people over the head with biblical standards in a way that drives them not to Christ and selfless living, but rather to frustration when they fail or pride when they think they don't"[9] (Crabb, 1991, p. 25).

Crabb sought to demonstrate that the problem is not merely in our woundedness, though that may be a problem, and it is not merely in a failure to apply biblical principles, though that also may be a problem; our biggest problem has to do with our "*justified* self-

---

[9] Quotations are taken from the 2013 edition.

centeredness" (Crabb, 1991, p. 62) and relational sin. Justified self-centeredness exists when someone acts out of a fearful, self-protective mindset, projecting blame on another for the way in which he or she has been treated. Rightly or wrongly, Crabb connected these first two approaches to relationship with egalitarianism and complementarism respectively. Regardless, it demonstrates his interest in gendered humanity, which he explored in later books in greater depth.

In the second half of the book, he explored genderedness in greater depth. He contended that men and women, though each image bearers, are fundamentally different from one another. He suggested that masculinity involves movement into the world whereas femininity tends to be invitational (Crabb, 1991, p. 142), yet each uniquely reflects aspects of the Trinity.

Finding God (1993)

Crabb's older brother Bill, his only sibling, was killed in a plane crash in 1991. *Finding God* (1993) was written out of that experience as Crabb was wrestling with intense personal suffering and loss. He has developed a reputation for his honesty and willingness to share his own personal struggles. *Finding God* was the first book in which he wrote deeply from an obvious place of brokenness, not as an expert, but as a pilgrim on the way. In this book, Crabb revealed the disorientation and gnawing confusion he felt about God.

Conventional wisdom suggests that pain reveals untapped resources that can be marshaled to effectively deal with pain ("whatever does not kill you makes your stronger"). Crabb's experience was different, however. Though pain may recruit some degree of inner fortitude, it more often reveals a deep-seated distrust of God and questions His goodness. It is easy to think "God first, family second, ministry third" when life is going well, but what about when pain and loss come?

In *Finding God* (1993), Crabb traced how a fundamental doubt about God's goodness often leads to an ultimately ineffectual pattern of dealing with pain that does not require helpless dependence on him. To the degree that we doubt God's goodness, we look for other "gods" that can be more easily controlled or domesticated. Because we are relational, these alternate gods usually take the form of other human beings. Because God appears to be unreliable, hurting people seek to meet their deepest longings through other people, increasing pressure on those relationships that can lead to hostility when disappointed. Alternatively, hurting people show self-contempt, finding that neither other people nor self ultimately relieve pain. In contrast to this broken structure, Crabb advocated a different process based on an imperfect, but quiet trust that God is fundamentally good, which creates space to love, rather than use, other people.

Suffering acutely reveals the fallen tendency to love created things more deeply than God. Quoting C.S. Lewis, Crabb wrote, "If I find in myself a desire which no experience in this world can satisfy, the most probable explanation is that I was made for another world" (1952/1980, p. 136). In addition to revealing our tendency to love other things more deeply than we love

God, pain heightens our sense of thirst, or longing, which Crabb addressed in both *Inside Out* (1988) and *Men and Women* (1991).

God of My Father (1994)

Like *The Adventures of Captain Al Scabbard* (1981), the biographical *God of My Father: A Son's Reflections on His Father's Walk of Faith* (1994) deviated from Crabb's typical focus on Christian psychology and soul care, though it did address relationships, a core theme for Crabb. However, he would be among the first to acknowledge that our principle relationships are formative. Written together with his father, *God of My Father* was the first book written after *Finding God* (1993) and reflected an awareness of the importance of family and an attestation to a faith that survived many difficult days. Though perhaps not a book of theoretical precision, *God of My Father* provides important insights into Dr. Crabb's own development as a Christian psychologist.

The Silence of Adam (1995/2013)[10]

In *The Silence of Adam: Becoming Men of Courage in a World of Chaos* (1995), Crabb (together with Don Hudson and Al Andrews) returned to the familiar themes of gendered spirituality and relationality. Reflecting on Genesis 3, Crabb asked the question "Where was Adam when the serpent tempted

[10] An updated and expanded edition of *The Silence of Adam* was re-released in 2013 by Zondervan under with the title *Men of Courage: God's Call to Move Beyond the Silence of Adam.*

Eve?...Why didn't he say anything?"[11] (p. 13). From the Genesis account, Crabb argued that men's failure to speak and move is the root of all their failures.

Traditional masculinity, as defined by contemporary culture and perhaps even by many men, consists of physical toughness, but too often is accompanied by relational weakness. In their silence, men fail to move toward other men and toward their families. Prompted by speaking engagements at the large Promise Keepers conferences, Crabb developed a vision of manhood built upon true godliness, a willingness to do something, and deep relationships. He wrote, "A man is most authentically a man when he admits, 'I don't know what to do in this situation, but I know it's important that I get involved and do something'" (Crabb, 1995, p. 63).

Crabb also expanded upon his understanding of what might be called relational holiness. He described our calling as the need "to reveal the unseen God by the way we live, especially by the way we relate to one another" (Crabb, 1995, p. 64). Increasingly, Crabb was becoming convinced of the importance of relationships and, in *The Silence of Adam*, suggested that men often struggled with this reality. Men were created to relate, but all bear the scars of Adam's silence with Eve in the garden. Crabb encouraged men to remember who they were created to be as masculine image bearers.

---

[11] Quotations are taken from the 2013 edition.

Connecting (1997)

Crabb considered *Connecting: Healing for Ourselves and Our Relationships* (1997) to be a turning point in his thinking and writing, representing his professional midlife crisis. In the introduction, he wrote, "The greatest need in modern civilization is the development of communities—true communities where the heart of God is home, where the humble and the wise learn to shepherd those on the path behind them, where trusting strugglers lock arms with others as they journey on" (p. xvii). Although these ideas were previously at the periphery of his thinking, with *Connecting* the necessity of community moved to the center.

Traditional modes of Christian counseling have tended toward one of two approaches: "exhortation and accountability," telling people what is wrong and what to do right, or "treatment and repair," where the goal is to diagnose what is psychologically wrong and deal with the damage, often with a trained psychotherapist (Crabb, 1997, pp. 32-34). The attentive reader will recognize that these themes were hinted at, though not fully developed, in earlier books, such as *Men and Women* (Crabb, 1991). Instead of these two traditional models, Crabb desired to see healing communities where people are reminded of God's goodness, the forgiveness of sin, and the freedom to indulge one's deepest desires (p. 38).

Again with a restless desire to be biblical, Crabb began to delve deeper into the Trinitarian nature of Christianity and, by extension, healing communities. As image bearers of a relational God, we were specifically designed to connect with God and one another and we are called to a life of other-centeredness, a theme that still shapes much of Crabb's current thinking.

The importance of vision also figured prominently in *Connecting*. Crabb began to explain that in healing communities, changes in thinking and behavior were secondary to developing a vision for who a person could become because of the gospel (Crabb, 1997, p. 66). This vision comes not from our own senses, but through sensitivity to what the Holy Spirit is doing in another's life. As we develop this vision, we ask: "What is the Spirit up to? What goodness is already in place and needs to be released?"

The Safest Place on Earth (1999)[12]

One of the themes that Crabb would become known for is his relationship with the church. We have already suggested that a theme that has permeated Crabb's writings, even from his earliest book, is his belief that soul care belongs to the church and not (primarily) to academically trained therapists. Yet out of this commitment grew a frustration with how he saw churches operating (2015). He witnessed little authentic relating actually happening in the church.

In *The Safest Place on Earth: Where People Connect and are Forever Changed* (1999), Crabb offered "a profound vision of what the church can be." In his estimation, churches too often have not been places

---

[12] *The Safest Place on Earth* was re-titled by Thomas Nelson in 2007 as *Becoming a True Spiritual Community: A Profound Vision of What the Church Can Be.*

where people relate deeply and authentically. They have failed to provide space where people can show curiosity about one another's journeys[13] (Crabb, 2007, p. 18) and where people are free to share safely about their lives, often because churches have been reluctant to acknowledge brokenness as a part of the fallen human condition. He wanted to see people develop a vision for others and feel the need to enter one another's lives, observe what is happening, and touch them deeply.

With specific regard to the Christian psychology project, Crabb addressed the question of whether psychology is good or bad. He wrote, "For guiding the church in providing soul care, I grant neither an authoritative nor a supplemental role to the discipline of psychology. I believe that empirical science and theoretical speculation must yield to special revelation and biblically dependent thinking in building a foundation and coming up with a strategy for this all-important work" (Crabb, 2007, p. 7).

Shattered Dreams (2001)

In *Shattered Dreams: God's Unexpected Path to Joy* (2001), Crabb returned to the topic of suffering and pain, first explored with some depth in his 1993 book, *Finding God*. He shared that (Crabb, 2015) his original contracted publisher rejected this book because of their belief that "few people will want to read about life's difficulties." Crabb was eventually able to contract with WaterBrook, who published *Shattered Dreams*. The

---

[13] Quotations are taken from the 2007 edition.

book was successful, lending support to the hypothesis that Crabb was writing about what people were actually experiencing.

Working from the book of Ruth, Crabb shared a higher vision for life than mere comfort. Many people presume that the abundant life consists of sufficient financial means, a few reasonably close friends, and generally good health, yet sometimes, Crabb contended, God allows dreams to shatter. How do people make sense of suffering? Crabb argued that suffering helps people to get in touch with a deeper longing for Christlikeness (cf. *Inside Out*, 1988).

Near the end of the book, Crabb shared a hopeful dream, "I long to experience the Presence of God moving through every detail of my life, both good details and bad ones, carrying me into a richer encounter with God, into a closer experience of community with others, and into an experience of personal transformation that makes me more like Christ" (Crabb, 2001, pp. 158-159). He is aware of the desire for satisfaction in God that will not be fully met in this lifetime, but that people long for. Awareness of that desire helps to foster a thirst for the Trinity.

The Pressure's Off (2002/2012)

In addition to thinking about Trinitarian relating, Crabb was increasingly focusing upon the importance of the new covenant for Christian believers. Romans 7:6 (New International Version), "But now, by dying to what once bound us, we have been released from the law so that we serve in the new way of the Spirit, and not in the old way of the written code," became foundational for Crabb's ministry activities. Indeed, when he founded *NewWay Ministries* in 2002, he named it at least in part based on his understanding of the new covenant from this verse. Although he touched on the new covenant in previous books such as *Becoming a True Spiritual Community* (Crabb, 1999) and *Shattered Dreams* (Crabb, 2001), he explored it much more deeply in *The Pressure's Off: Breaking Free from Rules and Performance* (2002).

In the introduction to the book, Crabb presented two paths. "Either you've decided that what you want most out of life is within your reach, and you're doing whatever you believe it takes to get it or, you've realized that what you want most is beyond your reach and you're trusting God for the satisfaction you seek. You want Him. Nothing less, not even his blessings, will do"[14] (Crabb, 2002, p. 11). This differentiation between old covenant and new covenant thinking is essential to understanding Crabb's later works. In his description of the new covenant here, you can also see that Crabb has been deeply affected by C.S. Lewis's idea that "You can't get second things by putting them first. You get second things only by putting first things first" (p. 280, Lewis, 1972).

An important idea presented in *The Pressure's Off* (2002) dealt with the problems associated the law of linearity (Crabb, 2002, p. 19). According to the law of linearity, if A happens, then B happens. It reflects the recipe theology Crabb had critiqued in the third chapter

---

[14] Quotations are taken from the 2012 edition.

of *Becoming a True Spiritual Community* (1999). He contrasted the law of linearity with what he described as the law of liberty, a restful experience of grace and reliance upon our faithful God by those who desire God as their supreme passion. The law of linearity, however, represents much of what constitutes modern psychotherapy. Crabb described the "adjustment cycle" and the "therapeutic cycle" as representative of old way thinking. In the "adjustment cycle" (Crabb, 2002, p. 176), one denies whatever they cannot handle, strategizes for a better life, evaluates how to make life work better, and then refines the plan as necessary. In the adjustment cycle, you control your destiny. Conversely, the "therapeutic cycle," often dressed up with Christian language moves from openness, to insight, to direction, to support, and eventually alignment of behavior with insight. Yet the therapeutic cycle remains a way of "using God to make your life work" (p. 179). Crabb contrasted these old ways of thinking with what he called the "spiritual cycle" (p. 180). In the spiritual cycle, a person begins with a sense of brokenness. From there, by the Spirit, they are led to repentance and abandonment to God. Once people abandon themselves to God, they become aware of an increased confidence in God's movement. This confidence in God in turn leads to releasing what is most alive. New Way living contrasts strongly with Old Way living, yet Crabb is convinced that it is the only way to live.

Soul Talk (2003)

In *Soul Talk: The Language God Longs for Us to Speak* (2003), Crabb presented a practical vision for his emerging thinking regarding community and spiritual direction. Reflecting concerns from earlier books, Crabb suggested that much of what constitutes conversations are simply self-talk, because people have failed to touch one another's souls.

In *Encouragement* (1994), Crabb differentiated between life words and death words, a theme that re-emerged here, albeit with a greater depth. He wrote, "most people go through their entire life never speaking words to another human being that come out of what is deepest within them, and most people never hear words that reach all the way into that deep place we call the soul" (p. 13). His vision for people is that we would develop a better understanding of what it means to speak life words to one another so that we might touch one another deeply.

Central to this book are the five stages of Soul Talk described by Crabb. The five stages are (p. 32):

1. **Thinking beneath**—What is happening beneath the surface of life? What is the real battle in another's soul?

2. **Thinking vision**—What is the Holy Spirit up to in another person's life?

3. **Thinking passion**—What is going on in my own soul as I speak?

4. **Thinking story**—What is their story? What do they value?

5. **Thinking movement**—How is the Spirit moving into a person's brokenness and leading them to grow more deeply in love with him and others?

Although the stages were introduced near the beginning, Crabb spent much of the book fleshing them out. Again, even a cursory observation may reveal how Crabb's thinking differs from much of what constitutes modern psychotherapy and, frankly, represented a significant shift relative to his earliest writings. *Soul Talk* (Crabb, 2003) provides a practical approach to living life in light of the Spirit, not in an effort to control another, but with an aliveness to what God is doing.

The PAPA Prayer (2006)

Though his writings increasingly focused upon relational holiness, sensitivity to the Holy Spirit, and conversations that matter, Crabb had yet to write a book on relating vertically with God through prayer. He admitted that he was a prayer struggler because it seemed as though prayers were so often left unanswered (Crabb, 2015). Continuing his focus upon the importance of relationship, *The PAPA Prayer: The Prayer You've Never Prayed* (2006) presented a method of relational prayer.

Crabb's disillusionment with prayer is not uncommon among believers. He began the book by asking several questions about the reader's experience with prayer. He asked questions such as whether people had ever prayed for something they didn't receive or whether it felt like God turned a deaf ear. Crabb suggested that although petitionary prayers may or may not be answered in the way we think, what he calls relational prayer always works because it is not about what people can get from God, but a way of being with God. "Relational prayer is the center of all true prayer" (Crabb, 2006, p. 32).

Briefly, Crabb presented relational prayer as involving four different movements: Present, Attend, Purge, and Approach (i.e., PAPA). In the PAPA prayer, a person begins by presenting themselves to God, talking about whatever is going on in them in the moment. In the second movement, a person, without pretense, pays attention to what they are thinking about God at the moment. Third, he or she brings out whatever might be blocking relationship with God (i.e., purge). Finally, he or she approaches God as the greatest good. A life in the New Way is in the process of transforming all aspects, including prayer, into deeper relational holiness.

66 Love Letters (2009a)[15]

Though not his best seller, *66 Love Letters: A Conversation with God that Invites You into His Story* (2009a) is arguably Crabb's magnum opus. He spent five years working on this book, which grew out of his desire to hear God speak. In the prologue, he shared his honest wrestling, something for which he has come to be known. He wrote, "I remember thinking, perhaps my responsibility is to believe He is speaking right now, and perhaps my job is to listen, maybe to see...Show me! Speak to me! I'm all eyes and ears" (p. xv). Yet no

---

[15] *God's Love Letters to You* (2010) was excerpted from *66 Love Letters* and offered as 40 day devotional.

visions, nor voices emerged. Crabb then realized, "God had already revealed Himself to me in His Son, and He had written a whole book to introduce His Son to me." (p. xv). He attempted to discern what God was speaking to him in each of God's 66 books, or love letters, a phrase he borrowed from Kierkegaard. The result was a series of "conversations" between Crabb and God revealing his honest questions and feelings (such as he talked about in The PAPA prayer) and God's response. Although not specifically marketed as a book of "spiritual direction," 66 Love Letters may be one of the most beneficial due to Crabb's living life in light of scripture and before a holy God. In 66 Love Letters, as a fellow believer, Crabb showed the reader what real life lived before God looks like.

Real Church (2009b)

In his earlier book about the church, The Safest Place on Earth (1995), Crabb addressed concerns about how Christians do church. Ten years later, he revisited the theme in Real Church: Does it Exist? Can I Find It? (2009b) as he asked himself, what kind of church he wanted to be a part of. He began, "Unplanned and unanticipated, this book jumped out of my personal disappointment, frustration, and concern with church as I've experienced it" (p. xv). Exploring his concerns, he offered suggestions about what church could be if it was built around four pillars (pp. xvii-xviii): 1) *spiritual theology*—a truth that touches souls rather than merely imparts facts; 2) *spiritual formation*—a dedication to become more deeply loving and other centered; 3) *spiritual community*—a desire to join together with others in Christ-like relating; and 4) *spiritual mission*—an outflow of formation and community into a world in need.

Having generally not found it, Crabb suggested that he wanted to be a part of a church where its people understand that they are all broken. He wrote, "I want to be a part of a church that knows two things clearly: 1) I am a mess, and 2) God is love" (Crabb, 2009b, p. 60). In light of these two points, Crabb spent much of the rest of the book exploring the themes of spiritual theology, spiritual formation, spiritual community, and spiritual mission.

Fully Alive (2013)

In *Fully Alive: A Biblical Vision of Gender that Frees Men and Women to Live Beyond Stereotypes* (2013), Crabb returned to the theme of gender, previously explored in some depth in *Men and Women* (Crabb, 1991) and *The Silence of Adam* (Crabb, 1995). In a culture struggling to make sense of sex and gender, Crabb began with the question, "What does it mean to be fully alive *as a male or female* for the glory of God?" (italics ours, Crabb, 2013, p. 14). From Crabb's perspective, neither the complementarian nor egalitarian points of view fully capture a biblical understanding of gender. Beginning with relational, Trinitarian assumptions, Crabb explored what gender revealed about how men and women relate to one another.

Crabb attempted to do the original languages justice. Noting that God referred to woman as *"neqebah"* in Genesis 1:27, which means "punctured, or bored through", he suggested that biblical femininity implied a relational openness and that they were created to invite rather than demand. A woman most fully alive to God then would be one who was inviting and open.

He worked from the Hebrew words *"zakar"* and *"arsen"* in trying to understand biblical masculinity. Zakar suggests remembrance and movement whereas arsen suggests carrying. He wrote, "Together arsen and zakar suggest the beginning idea that a man reflects God by remembering what is important and moving into a disordered situation with strength to make an important difference" (Crabb, 2013, p. 68). In *Fully Alive*, Crabb once again followed a third way, not clearly egalitarianism nor complementarism, to arrive at a compelling understanding of gender.

A Different Kind of Happiness (2016)

A Different Kind of Happiness: Discovering the Joy that Comes from Sacrificial Love (2016) is a clear distillation of Crabb's thinking about how to love well, reflecting four decades of growing wisdom regarding himself, God, and relationships. The "different kind of happiness" that Crabb wrote about here is a God-glorifying, other-centered happiness. He contended that true happiness is found in loving like Jesus, an idea that runs contrary to secular culture. Crabb admitted that no one, apart from Jesus, will ever love perfectly this side of heaven but that our journey toward Christlikeness is characterized by learning to love others more deeply, without any expectation of return. Though it is difficult to see, true happiness lies in suffering love.

The second part of the book described what Crabb called the "Seven questions of spiritual theology" (Crabb, 2016, p. 141). These seven questions distill much of the progression of his thinking over several decades. The questions are:

1. Who is God?
2. What is God up to?
3. Who are we?
4. What's gone wrong?
5. What has God done about our problem?
6. How is the Spirit working to implement the divine solution to our human problem?
7. How can we cooperate with the Spirit's work?

It becomes obvious when reading this section that Crabb has thought carefully about these questions. They reflect his Trinitarian understanding of God, the ongoing work of the Holy Spirit, the gendered, relational nature of image bearers, the sinful turn toward self-centeredness, and the opportunity to follow Christ on the narrow road.

When God's Ways Make No Sense (2018)

When reviewing Crabb's writing career, it is obvious that he does not shy away from difficult topics like suffering, gender, relational strain, and difficulties with church. He has consistently asked hard questions, inviting his readers to wrestle with them. In *When God's Ways Make No Sense* (2018), he asked how Christians are supposed to make sense of God in the midst of pain and confusion, when they may wonder whether God is even listening or when events seem to run so counter to God's revealed character. He suggested that when confronted with confusion about what God is up to, people have three options: resist and run, distort and deny, or tremble and trust. Crabb used the prophet Jonah as prototypical of someone who resisted God and ran from him. When God acted contrary to Jonah's expectations, rather than submitting to God's will, Jonah fled from God. Saul of Tarsus was his example of someone who distorted and denied the gospel message by reducing God's demands to what is achievable, and making it clear who was in and who was out of the kingdom of God. Crabb viewed each of these approaches as false ways to deal with confusion, encouraging his readers to look instead to Habakkuk, who trembled and trusted before the Lord. He wrote, "Don't pretend everything is to your liking when it is not. Face the hard truth that God may allow terrible suffering in the lives of people He loves for at least two reasons. One, to prod us into waiting eagerly with grateful anticipation for the trouble-free life we will forever enjoy in heaven, with Jesus. Two, to discover the Spirit's power to love like Jesus in any circumstance of life or condition of soul and thus to tell God's story of amazing grace" (p. 78). When life is hard, trust in the goodness of God.

As Crabb considered what God is up to in the midst of confusion of pain, he did not shy away from the inevitable questions regarding God's sovereignty. He suggested that there are three views of God's sovereignty. He identified the first as "meticulous sovereignty," a view that suggests that all things that happen are according to God's direct activity. According to the "contingent sovereignty" view, which he aligned with open theism, the future is allowed to unfold apart from God's awareness or control. Crabb rejected each of these options, preferring instead "unthwarted sovereignty," which rests on four propositions: 1) "God is free to do whatever He wishes," 2) "God is always active and up to something good," 3) "Even the wrath of man, energized by the flesh, directed by hell's wisdom, and approved by the world, will further God's eternal purpose to reveal Himself above all else as worthy of praise," and 4) "The sovereign God sees to it that nothing that happens in this world, nothing that either lost or saved people can do, will thwart his purpose" (pp. 204-205). Ultimately, according to this view, God is sovereign, and God is love.

Summary of Recurrent Themes

A review of Crabb's books highlights several themes which have developed over time. In his earliest works, including *Basic Principles of Biblical Counseling* (Crabb, 1975), *Effective Biblical Counseling* (Crabb, 1977), and *Marriage Builder* (Crabb, 1982), he began to develop a biblical understanding of human psychological functioning. His earliest works, in many regards, reflected a cognitive-behavioral understanding of meaningful change. Romans 12:1-2, dealing with the renewing of the mind, was a key passage for Crabb during those years.

However, over the course of his professional and personal life, his thinking matured. The centrality of thirst and longing, of relationship and other-centeredness, and of mystery and wisdom began to take prime positions in his writings. In light of personal circumstances, he began to explore how to suffer well. Over time, psychology became less prominent in regard to his professional identity, whereas the idea of spiritual direction increased. At this point in his career, his hope is to teach people to have meaningful conversations. Regardless, there are several themes that have emerged from our review of Crabb's work.

Model Building

From his earliest works, Crabb has worked hard to develop models for understanding of human psychological functioning. In *Basic Principles of Biblical Counseling* (Crabb, 1975), he provided basic descriptions of existing personality theories, which he contrasted with his own understanding of change. According to his early thinking, the process of change involved identifying negative feelings, negative behaviors, and negative thoughts, which are then changed through teaching that promotes right thinking and behavior and, subsequently, feelings that are satisfying (p. 47). He further developed and expanded this approach in *Effective Biblical Counseling* (Crabb, 1977).

As we discussed above, the model Crabb presented in *Understanding People* (Crabb, 1987) extended his earlier approach. He was more intentionally suggesting that although thoughts, feelings, and behavior were important, it was essential to consider personal variables, specifically that humans have longings that affect everything else. In this book, he also began to talk more freely about unconscious variables, putting his own spin on Freud's iceberg model (1963). "Above the waterline are conscious behaviors, beliefs, and emotions. Below the waterline is a network of images and beliefs that we choose to hold but that we refuse to identify clearly. We direct our lives according to a set of ideas of which we remain largely unaware" (p. 159). A few pages later (p. 163), he wrote that two of the major unconscious elements are relational pain and self-protective relational strategies, foreshadowing a significant part of his future work.

In *Inside Out* (1988), Crabb explored these sub-waterline themes more fully. He discussed the difference between crucial, critical, and casual longings that reside in each person and which affect our functioning. An inside look, a growing awareness of the effect of these longings, becomes critical in moving toward psychological health. Now, he was writing not only about changes in his thinking, nor just about change in relationships, but a fundamental change in the direction of being, learning to move into the world because of the power of Christ (p. 245).

As we discussed earlier, *Connecting* (Crabb, 1997) revealed a significant shift in his thinking, which was observable in his discussion of models of change. Pushing back against the accountability/exhortation model and the psychological therapy model, he suggested that the goal of helping is to release what is good in another by connecting in community and developing a vision for what another person may become. He continued to build upon the thinking described in *Connecting* in *The Pressure's Off* (2002) where he suggested that to live life in the New Way of the Spirit, one must reflect on where they are (i.e., the "red-dot principle"), understand their brokenness, admit they've been living for comfort rather than to glorify God, receive grace in humility, and desire to live to know God (pp.159-161). In *Soul Talk* (2003) and *The PAPA Prayer* (2006), he expanded his increasingly relational model in horizontal relationships with others and in our vertical relationship with God.

Role of the Church

Although his view of the church may at times have seemed unclear, it is fair to say that Crabb has always been pro-church and has specifically advocated for the importance of the church in providing soul care. In the opening to *Basic Principles of Biblical Counseling* (1975), Crabb wrote "I am convinced that the local church should and can successfully assume responsibility within its ranks for restoring troubled people to full, productive, creative life" (p. 16). A great deal of his life and ministry has been committed to pursuing this ideal. Indeed, the latter part of his career has largely been dedicated not to the training of professional counselors, but rather, to the equipping of non-professionals, members of local churches, desiring to connect with others.

Without question, the two books Crabb wrote specifically about the church made some people wonder whether he was anti-church. However, in both *The Safest Place on Earth* (1999) and *Real Church* (2009b), he shared his higher vision for what the church might become. In each case, he reflected upon the often shallow nature of the church and encouraged a deepening of what church might become, a community of fellow strugglers committed to loving well.

Gender

The understanding of gender is important in Crabb's work. He has consistently explored what it means to reflect the image of God as a gendered image bearer and how that is a source of joy when we operate from that view (Crabb, 1988, p. 53). In three books, Crabb specifically dealt with gender: *Men and Women* (1991), *The Silence of Adam* (1995), and *Fully Alive* (2014). He consistently demonstrated how maleness and femaleness are unique in terms of how we relate to others and bring glory to God; men remember and move, women open and invite. The core terrors of men and women subsequently reflect these biblical roles. A man's core terror is weightlessness (Crabb, 2013, p. 104) whereas a woman's core terror is an invitation with no response (Crabb, 2013, p. 90). In addition to these books, Crabb writes often of masculinity and femininity. Most recently, question #3 (Who are we?) of the seven questions of spiritual theology discussed in detail in *A Different Kind of Happiness* (Crabb, 2016) suggests that we are not just God's image bearers, but that we are *gendered* image bearers. Further, Crabb's wife Rachael together with Diana Calvin and Sonya Reeder published *Listen In: Building Faith and Friendships Through Conversations that Matter* (2015), which applied these ideas in female friendships.

Suffering

Crabb frequently deals with suffering. Throughout his life, and especially as he has faced his own losses, he has written meaningfully about suffering. In his writings, Crabb suggests that suffering is not something we escape from prior to heaven, but rather is something that comes to each person in varying degree and is an opportunity to glorify God.

Certainly, in *Finding God* (Crabb, 1993), *Shattered Dreams* (Crabb, 2002), and *When God's Ways Make No Sense* (Crabb, 2018), Crabb has helped readers to grapple with suffering in the normal Christian life. However, its presence is ubiquitous. Even in his 1984 book *Encouragement* (Crabb & Allender, 1984), prior to the loss of his job at Grace Seminary, the death of his brother, the loss of his parents, or his battles with cancer, he demonstrated an awareness of the impact of suffering. He wrote, "The route to knowing God eventually passes directly through the valley of profound loneliness. It is in the times when there is no one but God that we learn to know him most fully" (p. 69). For Crabb, suffering enhances our awareness of thirst. The questions raised in his most recent book, *When God's Ways Make No Sense* rest firmly in the confusion of a world where God seems absent and evil reigns.

The Trinity

Undoubtedly, this theme and the next, the new covenant, are crucial to understanding Crabb's current thinking. Crabb wrote, "Final reality is relational. Our highest calling is to love as directed by the Holy Spirit who is the embodiment of the loving relationship between the Father and the Son, a love so alive that the Spirit is Himself an eternal, divine Person. God's plan is to conquer evil by suffering, sacrificial love, centered in Christ's death, followed by our living relationally as 'slaughtered lambs'" (Crabb, 2015). One cannot understand Crabb's thinking without a deep appreciation of the importance of Trinitarian relating.

Although central to his current thinking, the importance of relationship has been present throughout his career. Crabb has frequently described that typically at the heart of human suffering is relational breakdown, or what he has frequently described as relational sin. As a result of the fall, we tend to be self-centered and self-protective. In order to try to avoid pain, we fail to love. "Everyone develops a style of relating designed to avoid the experience of deep personal pain, and that is the sin of self-protection...When the demand for self-protection interferes with our willingness to move toward others with their well-being in view, the law of love is violated" (Crabb, 1988, p. 141).

But relational holiness and biblical love are other-centered. In *The Marriage Builder,* Crabb described love as a "preoccupation with the *other's* needs" (Crabb, 1982, p. 69). This other-centeredness often comes with cost to self. "Kingdom living consists of radical servanthood (the end of entitlement to personal comfort) and self-denying suffering with the hope of joy forever" (Crabb, 2009a, p. 214-215). In modern Western society, the call to radical other-centeredness is countercultural. The cultural tide says that individuals must prioritize their own needs and comfort over and above anyone else's, whereas Crabb contends that truly biblical love is self-sacrificial. Perhaps an even more radical thought is that *true* happiness may be found only in other-centered love. "First thing happiness, in God's thinking a better kind of happiness, develops when we struggle to love others with a relationship of costly love that is possible only if we have a life-giving relationship with Jesus that is grounded entirely in His love for us" (Crabb, 2016, p. 20).

As we begin to understand Jesus's love for us, and that He wants us to love one another the way He and the Father love one another (cf. John 17), we become free to love and relate perichoretically. In the same way that the Father pours into the Son and the Son into Father, "when God created us in His image, He intended that we would similarly pour into one another from the deepest resources of our being" (Crabb & Allender, 1985, p. 105). Crabb continued, "More than anything else, we were built to enjoy relationship, the kind that the Trinity has always enjoyed and extends to sinful people" (p. 171).

New Covenant

Together with his focus on Trinitarian relating, an understanding of the new covenant is foundational to understanding Crabb's ideas. Believers under the new covenant now have a new heart because of Christ and a new power because the Holy Spirit living within them provides a way to live and love like Christ. In that context, when we fail to live consistent with our identity as new covenant believers, we sin relationally, "falling short of the *relational glory* of the Trinity" (Crabb, 2015).

Crabb first addressed the importance of the new covenant in *The Safest Place on Earth* (Crabb, 1999) where he stated that the new covenant provided believers with "a new way to relate" (p. 107) out of an understanding of our "new purity" and "new identity," which gave us a "new inclination" that we could follow due to a "new power"—the four provisions of the new covenant (p.108ff). New covenant believers live with freedom, by the power of the Spirit, in self-sacrificial love for God and others. Not only were we *created* to relate as God's image bearers, but because of the new covenant we are also *able* to relate.

Concluding Thoughts

So far, Larry Crabb's writing career has spanned over four decades during which he has written 26 books, the majority revealing his lifelong commitment to Christian psychology. His professional development has, in many ways followed the course of his personal life. His "agile mind" (a term offered by his father while he was in college) and exceptional graduate training prepared him for the rigors of work as a professional psychologist. Yet no one is separable from their background. Crabb's early formation under the watch of the church and godly parents provided an important foundation for his future development. Throughout his life, the loss of loved ones, occupational stresses, bouts with cancer, and relational discord shaped his thinking as well. Through all of this, however, he has remained doggedly committed to seeking the God who was seeking him and generations of readers have, and will continue to, benefit from his willingness to honestly grapple with hard questions.

Now in his 70s, God alone knows what the future holds for Dr. Crabb. In sharing his vision for the future, he shows few signs of slowing down. He wrote, "I desire to continue schools for spiritual direction, writing books, and preparing video curriculum" (Crabb, 2015). In fact, in 2019, Larry and his son Kep have begun to release webinars through *Larger Story*, a not-for-profit ministry started by Kep[16]. Larry's passion is palpable; his wisdom, expansive; and his mind, as sharp as ever. Lord willing, future generations of Christian psychologists, church leaders, and believers of all stripes will take the time to read his works. His message for the church and the world still needs to be heard, as consistently and clearly as ever.

---

[16]largerstory.com

RICHARD E. AVERBECK

GOD, PEOPLE, AND RELATIONSHIP THROUGH THE LENS OF SCRIPTURE

L arry Crabb and I have been friends and colleagues for over 35 years. When he began teaching at Grace Theological Seminary in 1981, I was a new professor in the Old Testament department there, having finished my Ph.D. course work in OT and ancient Near Eastern (ANE) studies at Dropsie College in Philadelphia. I still had my dissertation to write, but had begun teaching full-time the previous year. As he and Dan Allender started their counseling program, I was teaching Old Testament studies to their students and those in the Master of Divinity program as well. There was a good deal of controversy in those days over Christian counseling and psychology – not just at Grace, but nationally and globally. Some of the faculty at Grace were in support of the counseling program whereas others were not. Sometime in the first week or two of his time at Grace, I walked into Larry's office to let him know that I was glad he was there. His response was, "Why?" That was how our relationship started. His wife (Rachael) and mine (Melinda) became friends as well, and we developed a good relationship as couples that endures to this day. Their friendship has had a profound impact on us.

In the first years at Grace, Melinda and I started our family, while I finished my Ph.D. degree and taught full-time. It was a very busy season of life, but not too busy for me to participate in a faculty group led by Larry and Dan. Not long ago, I confirmed with Larry that back then he took me on as "a project," so to speak. As for me, I was truly curious about what makes people tick, and he seemed to know something about that. I had no idea, however, what it would look like to reach deeply into another person's life, or let them into mine. That includes my wife, which is a point that Larry once brought home to me in a powerful and transforming way. After finishing my Ph.D., I immediately began the M.A. in counseling program under Larry and Dan, and Tom Varney also, who had joined their team by that time.

This background is essential to my interaction with this very discerning summary of Larry Crabb's career by Jason Kanz and Bryan Maier. Larry is powerful in the way he thinks and just as much in the way he relates to people around him day by day. The core of his thinking finds its source in the Bible as he contemplates God, people, and the relationship between the two, which has had a significant effect on me. With Larry's ongoing influence, it occurred to me that I needed to rethink my work in the Bible, specifically in relation to what I was finding in working with people. The goal would be to keep going deep into both the Bible and the lives of people, and build a biblical theology from the intersection between the two. The core of this rethinking first began to develop during Larry's supervision of my internship in the counseling program at Grace, and it continues up to this day (Averbeck, 2006; 2008).

As Kanz and Maier have rightly noted, there have been a number of shifts in Crabb's perspective through the years; for example, from right thinking to good relating. It is not as if he left one behind for the other, however. His understanding has accumulated progressively with a good deal of ongoing continuity. He has often been disillusioned and critical of the church, for example, but not in a way that dismissed it. Dr. Crabb has always believed that the healthy local church community should be the place for Christians to find the help they need. What makes for such "health" in the church is the kind of "soul talk" among the people that Crabb has written about (Crabb, 2003). Shallow relationships make for shallow Christians and shallow churches that do not minister to the deeper needs of their people.

In my view, Kanz and Maier have done us a real service in their essay, but there are certain points that could use further clarification. I am thinking here especially about their review of Dr. Crabb's move into spiritual formation and spiritual direction from

Christian counseling. It is natural for Kanz and Maier to put more emphasis on Crabb as a Christian counselor, especially in the context of Christian psychology. That, however, is the point at issue. Crabb's progressively developing model of counseling is what eventually led him to take up spiritual formation and direction, and to follow his own course in doing so. As I see it, this was the natural and biblically logical end of his long-term dogged pursuit of truth. Larry Crabb was born for spiritual formation and direction, and I have told him so. In effect, it has brought him to a place where he puts a proper and profound emphasis on the work of the Holy Spirit in and through the believer in the community of faith.

It is probably important to note the fact that Dr. Crabb is still commonly mentioned in books on approaches to psychology and Christian counseling, but no longer as a major player in the ongoing developments in the field (e.g., the author indices in Johnson and Myers, 2010; Jones & Butman, 2011; Greggo & Sisemore, 2012), which appears to be a natural result of his shift away from Christian counseling to spiritual formation and direction. This is where he is putting his major focus and energy these days. If one were to place Crabb within the current trends in the field of Christian counseling, however, he would have the most in common with the approach label as "transformational," because this approach to Christian counseling naturally draws upon spiritual formation and direction, and the soul care traditions of the church.

Dr. Crabb practices and teaches what he calls the Passion/Wisdom Model of Spiritual Direction. On the one hand, he draws on the ancient and enduring spiritual formation and soul care tradition of the church through his reading and personal relationships with leaders in that field, for example, his good friend James Houston – one of the patriarchs of the spiritual formation movement in North America, a mentor to many, and former professor of spiritual theology at Regent College in Vancouver, Canada. On the other hand, Crabb's form of spiritual direction also draws deeply from the well of his earlier thinking as a Christian counselor. This is another expression of the progressive accumulation and continuity in his thinking through the years. He is concerned with how people think and how they relate to God and the people in their lives, and wants us to do "soul talk" with one another specifically about these matters. This would include, for example, looking at and working through the experiential, cognitive, and relational roots of personal sin. It will also involve viewing people as both agents and victims of corruption. These have been points of emphasis, and often contention, with other approaches to psychology and Christian counseling, since early in his career.

As Kanz and Maier have noted, Crabb started his career as an "integrationist" of sorts. The problem as I see it is what one means by "integration." Crabb called it "spoiling the Egyptians." In Crabb's view, psychological theory and research has real value in the world of Christian counseling, but he places it under the authority of the Bible. If something from psychology does not fit under the umbrella of biblical thinking, it does not belong in Christian counseling (see also Eck, 2007; Entwistle, 2015). He has never been happy with what integration means for many in the field, and often shies away from the term altogether. Some writers and practitioners, for example, essentially put the Bible and secular psychological theory and research on equal footing (i.e., the "two book" theory), although they might prioritize the Bible when it comes to moral values and such. It is of course true that the Bible does not deal with every specific issue that modern psychology does, but the fact of the matter is that the Bible does indeed deal with the reality and the roots of the human dilemma from which all these issues arise. Of course, Crabb also takes into consideration that there are sometimes organic issues that come into play, which may require medical intervention.

Larry Crabb has always shown special interest in issues of male and female, and the relationship between the two. Although his Hebrew word etymologies are not so convincing to me (e.g., Crabb, 2013), he has always had an uncanny sense of femaleness and maleness, and how God intends for a man and a woman to relate to one another in a marriage relationship. I agree that his work in this area is "compelling," as Kanz and Maier put it.

Kanz and Maier rightly emphasize throughout their review that Crabb is a man of the Bible. In fact, Dr. Crabb is a fantastic Bible teacher, and he is perhaps the most powerful communicator I know. He is fully committed to the Bible as an essentially relational book, and the fact that in it we find God's special revelation of how we have been created for relationship with him and one another. In recent years, Dr. Crabb has focused a good deal of attention on the relationships within the Trinity – Father, Son, and Holy Spirit – and their importance for our understanding of good interpersonal relating. Trinitarian awareness is not new with Dr. Crabb, of course. Theologians and biblical scholars have been pursuing this subject for a long time, and there has been a strong push in this direction for the last thirty years or so in particular. Where Crabb is especially effective, however, is in his emphasis on the fact that God not only created us for relationship, but has also enabled us to relate to one another and God in a Trinitarian way through the provisions of the new covenant.

When considering the new covenant, there is a danger of pitting the NT against the OT. After all, God did not wait to start working relationally in the lives of people until the time of the new covenant. Jesus's two great commandments come from the OT Law (Matthew 22:34-40 and parallels), God gave the Law at Sinai to be a guide and enablement for them to live well as a nation in covenant with God (Deuteronomy 30:11-20); even the new covenant does not leave the OT Law behind, but writes it on the heart (Jeremiah 31:33). Moreover, although there are some differences, the Holy Spirit worked in lives of believers in the OT too, not just since the time of Jesus and the NT (Averbeck, 2005). It is important to keep remembering that the Apostle Paul thought of the law as a good thing, holy, righteous, and even spiritual (Romans 7:12-14). He did not want his hearers to disregard the Law even as he highlighted the weakness of the Law as compared to the Spirit (Romans 7:7-11; 8:2-4). The Holy Spirit can change the heart of a person; the Law cannot. God did not design the Law for that purpose in the first place. He gave the Law as a good and holy guide to people whose hearts have already been changed by the work of the Holy Spirit producing Abrahamic faith and faithfulness in them (Genesis 15:6 with Romans 4 and Galatians 3; see also Romans 8:14-39).

That said, however, what God showed us and did for us in Jesus Christ is absolutely without parallel for all time and eternity. Dr. Crabb has wonderfully pointed the way to living life well in Jesus according to the will of the Father by the enabling power of the Holy Spirit in the community of faith. Crabb has enriched us with his life and his thinking, and the highly articulate and motivating ways he has presented it to us. For over forty years, he has labored hard and with good effect for counselors and the people they counsel, for people of faith and their communities of faith, and above all, for the God to whom he has devoted his life, and whom he continues to pursue with deep and abiding passion. Thankfully, he is not done yet! Praise be to God!

BRUCE DEMAREST

A THEOLOGICAL AND FORMATIONAL REFLECTION

Thanks to Drs. Kanz and Maier for their excellent summary of Dr. Crabb's career and the development of his thought and ministry over the decades. I appreciate the invitation to participate in this tribute to Dr. Crabb with whom I have been privileged to share a few teaching ministries in the Denver area. The following comments will focus on areas of my interest and training, namely, theological, formational, and soul care aspects of Dr. Crabb's current thought.

Professional Psychology and Soul Care

Reflecting on the three counseling models presented in the summary, my mind turned to Genesis 1:27-28 which undergirds the so-called "cultural mandate," whereby God commands image-bearers to cultivate the created order for the good of humankind. Theologian Emil Brunner proposed the "law of closeness of relation"

(Brunner, 1946, p. 383), which states that the closer a discipline approaches the core of the religious life, the greater is the distortion due to sin. Thus, a Baptist and a Buddhist can be expected to arrive at the same answer to a mathematical problem, but broad divergences occur in the disciplines of psychology, philosophy, and theology due to conflicting world views and sin's effects on the mind. Consistent with Brunner's maxim, over the years Dr. Crabb rightfully has become less confident of secular models of psychology and less reliant on integrationists' use of secular theories.

I celebrate Dr. Crabb's acceptance of the valid findings of psychology and his acknowledgment that in areas where the Bible does not speak "we may look to other sources of information for help" (Crabb, 1987, p. 48). On the other hand, I delight in his conviction that special revelation in Scripture governs the theory and practice of soul care. His thought converges with the discipline of "spiritual theology" developed by authorities such as Simon Chan (1998) and Eugene Peterson (2005). Concerning the model of "biblical psychology," a brief Crabbian response would have been helpful since evangelicals uphold the sufficiency of Scripture in all matters of faith and life. Dr. Crabb's does observe, however, that "there is more to real counseling than rebuke and exhortation" (Crabb, 1975, p, 50).

I concur with Dr. Crabb's insistence that soul care is best exercised within the community of the local church. Many soul maladies brought to therapists may be remediated by the life-giving protocols of spiritual formation and soul care. When conflicted souls are taught how to live out the fruit of the Spirit and exercise agape love, lasting change occurs. In our church community, the Sunday school or Christian education model has been replaced by a spiritual formation hour with positive outcomes.

Nature of the Human Person

Two aspects of Dr. Crabb's perspective on the human person invite comment. Whereas Dr. Crabb's early perspective emphasized cognitive and behavioral functioning, his later thought wisely emphasizes deep desires and longings. Illicit desires can be transformed solely by divine grace which illumines the mind and empowers the will to pursue holiness and love with resultant soul satisfaction.

I further celebrate his conviction that essentially persons are relational beings. Christian theology in recent decades has reasserted that relationality is a dominant feature of humanness. Wisely, Dr. Crabb eschews the reductionist position that relationality is the sole determinant of humanness. His enhanced understanding of human relationality is evident in his robust emphases on human community, connecting with others at a deep level, and shepherding others via biblical soul care protocols.

Quite independently, my experience has paralleled Dr. Crabb's. Two decades ago, needing spiritual refreshment, I enrolled in a six-week residential program in spiritual formation and direction at a Spirit-filled renewal community in New Mexico. A surprising grace of this experience was the powerful sense of community which made existentially real the experience of the apostolic community described in the early chapters of Acts. My life-changing journey in the Benedictine community is chronicled in the book, *Satisfy Your Soul: Restoring the Heart of Christian Spirituality* (Demarest, 1999). The transforming inner journey of engaging my heretofore unexplored inner being—what Augustine called the journey to one's inner Sinai—led to an outer journey of spiritual formation and soul care ministered in my local church, seminary community, and wider world.

The Relational Trinity

I further celebrate Dr. Crabb's emphasis on the relational Trinity as foundational for soul care ministry. His thought integrates three essential findings of theology: (a) that Trinitarian life is characterized by mutuality, co-belonging, and complete sharing (John 17:10); (b) that a profound allocentricity characterizes Trinitarian relations, namely, that each divine person promotes the significance of the others (John 17:1, 4, 5); and; (c) that unconditional love exists between the three divine persons (John 3:35; John 17:25). Dr. Crabb effectively highlights the ancient Christian doctrine of *perichoresis*, which affirms the mutual indwelling of the three persons of the Trinity such that the supernatural life of each flows through the others (John 17:21).

I would add that Christ-followers are not only summoned to *model* the inter-Trinitarian relations, but more radically we are personally and collectively *caught up* into the loving, relational life of the Trinity. Since all believers are united "in Christ" (2 Corinthians 5:17), we are vitally united with one another (cf. 2 Peter 1:4). Thus profoundly interrelated, disciples together live out the self-giving, self-communicating, always-loving Trinitarian life wherein the divine life is poured into others. I would add that emphasis on the relational Trinity might be enriched by appeal to the wisdom of classical spiritual authorities; for example, the fertile insights of Teresa of Avila's transforming union with the Trinity and with one another portrayed in mansions six and seven of her *Interior Castle* (1979, pp. 108-194).

Revaluation of Prayer

Dr. Crabb's dictum in *The PAPA Prayer* (2006) that petitionary prayer may lead to disillusionment when answers are not forthcoming but that relational prayer always works, is insightful. His mature understanding that "Relational prayer is the center of all true prayer" (p. 32) represents a corrective to the typical view of prayer as petition offered to God. In his *Institutes of the Christian Religion*, Calvin insisted that prayer is more than petition. The Reformer urged "right & pure contemplation of God" (Calvin, 1960, 3.20.4), adding that "The best prayers are sometimes unspoken." (3.20.33).

Agreeable with Dr. Crabb, relational prayer involves abiding in God's presence, resting in his love, and responding to God's gentle Spirit with confession, thanksgiving, and adoration. Richard Baxter (d. 1691), the English non-conformist, noted that contemplation "opens the door between the head and the heart" and "presents to the affections those things that are most important." He judged that the Reformers overreacted to Rome by abandoning contemplative prayer and related disciplines. "If God's Word be so full of consolation," he added, "what overflowing springs should we find in God Himself?" (Baxter, 1998, pp. 547ff.).

The PAPA form of prayer reflects the relational emphasis historically known as contemplation. Thomas Merton stated that contemplation is an engagement "by which we know and love God as He is in Himself, apprehending Him in a deep and vital experience which is beyond the reach of any natural understanding . . ." (Merton, 1979, p. 144). Similarly, M. Basil Pennington defines contemplation as "an opening, a response, a putting aside of all the debris that stands in the way of our being totally present to the present Lord, so that he can be present to us." (Pennington, 1980, p. 86).

Dr. Crabb's relational emphasis on prayer is both historically attested and biblical (Psalm 27:4). Mary reposed at Jesus's feet with heart focused on him (Luke 10:39) as well as John leaning on Jesus's breast in the Upper Room (John 13:23, 25) support the PAPA emphasis. As an aside, I find Paul's command to "pray continually" (1 Thessalonians 5:17) intriguing, and speculate how Dr. Crabb might interpret this command since not even a monk ensconced in a cave can pray verbally without ceasing.

Suffering, Formation, and Soul Care

Dr. Crabb rightly wrestles with the greatest obstacle to a trusting relationship with God, namely, the magnitude of human suffering. Correctly, he maintains that God never promised to eliminate pain and suffering, but to be with his people in the midst of their trials. Radical discipleship means following Jesus who experienced pain, disappointment, and rejection. Dr. Crabb would agree that Christians must remember that we follow the *crucified* Lord. Follow-ship of Jesus and suffering are joined at the hip.

Consistent with his emphasis on longing and desire, Dr. Crabb makes the important point that suffering stimulates thirst for God and Christlikeness as well as trust in his providence. Wisely, he counsels that sufferers must not become bitter and cynical, but trust God's wisdom for permitting suffering with its potential for soul transformation. With the prop of self-sufficiency torn away, sufferers are motivated to surrender to God and His will (1 Peter 4:19) and to seek spiritual support in the *koinonia* of the body (Galatians 6:2). Dr. Crabb astutely observes that suffering begets compassion, which reaches out to others in need.

My thinking has followed a path similar to Dr. Crabb's in the sense that the distressing sense of God's absence and consequent loneliness creates a void in the heart which kindles desire for him. His reflections on suffering (cf. the dark night of the soul) remind me of Mother Teresa, who testified to being in a distressing dark night for five decades while caring for the destitute in Calcutta. Aided by discerning spiritual directors, she understood that the darkness was purifying her imperfections, deepening love for Jesus, and intensifying her compassion. Mother Teresa believed that by serving in the darkness she might become the light of Jesus to the unwanted and unloved who were languishing in their night of unbelief (Mother Teresa, 2007).

Summation

I appreciate the remarkable way in which Dr. Crabb's thinking has evolved over the years. I value his willingness to challenge the psychological establishment with the truths of biblical revelation and his emphasis on the profoundly relational nature of the human person. I celebrate his insight into the Trinity as the ultimate paradigm of intimacy with God and mutual relating as well as his perspective on prayer as life-giving engagement with the living God. I likewise resonate with his perspective on the transformative nature of human suffering. Dr. Crabb's admission that that his thinking on formation and soul care remain a work in progress testifies to the reality that we never arrive, but are always arriving. The trajectory of his mature thought—refined through clinical practice, controversy, and the challenges of personal suffering—brings us much closer to a biblical and historically Christian understanding of the counseling enterprise, spiritual formation, and soul care.

COLIN DYE

A MASTER EXPONENT OF THE INNER LIFE

The authors have given a helpful review of Crabb's thought expressed in his writings over the past four decades. Of particular value is the way the authors show how Crabb's later works follow naturally from the insights and concerns of his earlier material. When comparing *Effective Biblical Counseling* (1977) and *Understanding People* (1987) with the later works, *Soul Talk* (2003) and *A Different Kind of Happiness* (2016), one could be tempted to think that Crabb had experienced a *volte face* in his thinking sometime in the 1990s[17]. One could conclude that Crabb had rejected counseling as a professional discipline in favour of a more classical approach to Christian spirituality evident in his Soul Care model. This would be a superficial judgment, however, as the authors have ably

---

[17] The authors acknowledge that Crabb's book, *Connecting* (1997) represented a significant shift in his thinking.

demonstrated. The seeds of Crabb's thought are shown to develop and finally blossom in his more recent works. The focus on the inner life, the importance of Trinitarian understanding, brokenness, knowing God as the highest good, loving God and others as the priority for Christians, and the value of deep, spiritual relationships in the community of God's people – all these develop and progressively flourish in Crabb's works.

Negative responses

The authors make reference to the negative response Crabb has sometimes received from Christian counselors. Some accused him of compromising biblical teaching by depending on secular psychology. I first met Dr. Crabb in the mid 1980's as he gave seminars in the UK on the material that would be finally published in *Understanding People* (1987). A few years before, I had been introduced to Nouthetic Counseling and also had attended various seminars held in the UK. Some Nouthetic Counselors considered Crabb's approach to be a Christianised version of Albert Ellis's Rational Emotive Therapy. The authors point out that Crabb was critical of secular psychological theories in *Basic Principles of Biblical Counseling* (1975) and secular therapeutic models in *Effective Biblical Counseling* (1977). They also cited Crabb's assertion of the Bible's authority over and against divergent psychology even when seemingly supported by empirical research in *Becoming a True Spiritual Community* (1999). This together with Crabb's consistent attempts to be thoroughly biblical in his consideration of all matters relating to life, effective living, and the human condition ought to have satisfied his critics (Crabb, 1987). But the discussion continued, taking various forms as the Biblical Counseling movement developed (Lambert, 2012).

Crabb was himself cautious of the nouthetic counseling approach that seemed too easily conformed to a Christianised version of Moral Therapy or William Glasser's Reality Therapy. He wanted to pay attention to issues "beneath the water line" (cf. *Inside Out,* 1988). He developed a credible personality theory consistent with the scriptural teaching on humanity created as gendered image bearers, the fall, redemption, sanctification, Christian community, and the future life.

The authors acknowledge the apparent similarity between Crabb's earlier counseling model and Cognitive Behaviour Therapy. They also show that in subsequent writings, Crabb moved away from a primarily cognitive-based approach, increasingly highlighting the importance of fundamental human longings. This was in part the result of Crabb's attempts to clarify his position as well as a development in his understanding. According to Crabb, his frequent references to "having our needs met" was considered by some people as tantamount to promoting "a man-centered focus on fulfillment rather than a God-centred emphasis on obedience to Him and preoccupation with His glory" (Crabb, 1987). This was the very thing Crabb was at pains to avoid. Lovingly and graciously, Crabb refined his language, nuanced his assertions, and clarified his position: "Because my choice of the term 'need' has apparently communicated to a few what I do *not* believe and what I strongly oppose, I hope that referring to 'deep longings that constitute the thirst for what our Lord can alone quench' will better convey what I have always believed" (emphasis in original, 1987/2013, p. 18).

The Emergence of a Soul Care Model

The authors rightly highlight Crabb's commitment to devising models of human personality and people-helping. Crabb views them as helpful tools for understanding and communication, but not a rigid pattern to follow. In my church in London, the pastoral team adapted Crabb's earlier counseling model for our own counseling ministry. We maintained the three levels of counseling engagement proposed in *Effective Biblical Counseling* (1977): encouragement, exhortation, and enlightenment. We trained church members and lay leaders to engage in the level appropriate to their gifts and calling.

In recent years, however, we connected with Crabb's Soul Care and Spiritual Direction approach. In many ways, it was a departure from the more technical professional-client approach of former years. The goal was now to equip every believer to be a companion of others on the journey toward knowing God. The authors rightly underscore Crabb's consistent support of the church and his view of the Christian community being the primary crucible for testing and developing our love for God and our neighbours. The sheer beauty of this approach is that every member of the church can engage in it. The Passion-Wisdom model emerged out of

Crabb's growing emphasis on relational theology and his commitment to enabling the body of Christ to engage in meaningful, in-depth communication with one another. Crabb continues to grow, push boundaries, and disturb the spiritually comfortable. In particular, his concept of human beings as "fallen gendered image-bearers" is far reaching, and may yet prove to be a bedrock of understanding as society grapples with new challenges to traditional views of sexuality and gender. Principally, Larry focuses on gender as a God-given relational identity. He uses the term "gendered image bearers." This means we cannot approach the gender issue merely in terms of roles or rights in society and in the church, still less in terms of cultural stereotypes. Larry helps us see gender as a fundamentally spiritual identity, the expression of which is essential to human flourishing and to our relationship with God and others. This is a valuable contribution to the debate and has the potential to shape future discussion.

Is the non-professional approach adequate?

An important question remains: does Crabb's approach do away with the need for clinical psychology and psychiatry? To my knowledge, Crabb makes no such assertion. He simply wants to equip followers of Christ to develop meaningful spiritual relationships. His Soul Care model opens the way for members of the Christian community to develop their God-given relationships through in-depth scriptural understanding and participation in the Holy Spirit. This is clearly beyond the scope of the secular approaches. For Crabb, the goal

is to bring the church to spiritual maturity, not healing
per se. That goal remains a far off dream for many
leaders in pastoral ministry today, but Crabb has offered
significant signposts pointing churches in the right
direction.

Summary

I would summarise Crabb's contribution to the
understanding of human psychology by suggesting he is
a master exponent of the inner life. Not only do we find a
credible Christian psychology, but, more profoundly, a
Christian spirituality consistent with it. Crabb's teaching
is practical and anchored in real life. He continues to
agonise over the inherent self-centredness in us all. He
leads the way by ruthlessly exposing his own inner life in
his relentless pursuit of God. It remains a "road less
travelled", but many more are now able to tread that
path as Crabb continues to blaze the trail ahead of us.

MARK R. MCMINN

LIVING WITH GRACE IN A COMPLICATED WORLD

I am grateful to Jason Kanz and Bryan Maier for their fine essay about the lifetime contributions and writings of Larry Crabb, and especially to have opportunity to add to this conversation. Drs. Kanz and Maier admit in their first paragraph that their individual experiences with Dr. Crabb might influence their essay. I hope so. Dr. Crabb's way of being with others is entirely consistent with the words he has written, and so his interpersonal manner should also be part of how we celebrate his career and contributions. In the several interactions I have had with Dr. Crabb over the years, I have always left with a slightly lighter step, a more hopeful and enlivened experience of living in our complicated world, and a sense that I have encountered that sacred space where wisdom and grace flourish.

A Graduate School Encounter

My first experience with Dr. Crabb was through his second book, *Effective Biblical Counseling* (1977). I was a graduate student at Vanderbilt University at the time, completing my Ph.D. in clinical psychology despite having been warned by wise and caring people in my home church that studying psychology would likely cause me to lose my faith. That home church was a Plymouth Brethren assembly; I was surprised to learn from Kanz and Maier that Dr. Crabb's background was also Plymouth Brethren. During my first day on Vanderbilt's campus another psychology doctoral student heard a bit of my story, looked at me with shock, and said, "What? You can't possibly be religious and be a social scientist!" Maybe I'm stubborn, or perhaps I was just too far down the road to turn back, but I determined to move forward with both my doctoral degree and my faith, however lonely such a journey might be. Long before we ever met, Dr. Crabb was one of my few companions on that journey. *Effective Biblical Counseling* gave me hope that I could love God, hold a high view of scripture, and study psychology.

The Wheaton College Encounter

A number of years later, I had opportunity to meet Dr. Crabb, after he had authored several more books and become as famous as a Christian psychologist can become. I was a professor at Wheaton College teaching in their new Psy.D. program, and looking for someone to come speak at the annual featured integration event—

the Scandrette Lecture. We had only $400 to offer as an honorarium, and I knew we couldn't get Larry Crabb for that amount, but I had enough hubris to ask anyway. Dr. Crabb had recently published *Connecting* (1997), which spoke powerfully the role the church might play in addressing our deepest longings. Because the psychology department at Wheaton was in the process of launching a Center for Church-Psychology Collaboration, the fit seemed perfect even if the honorarium was woefully inadequate. To my great surprise, Dr. Crabb accepted the invitation.

On the way from my home in Wheaton to pick up Dr. Crabb at O'Hare Airport, I pondered an unfortunate encounter I had the year prior when sharing a cab ride with another famous Christian author. I felt so relieved to escape that taxi after our 20-minute ride because the author's narcissism was overwhelming and suffocating. Driving to O'Hare, I found myself hoping and praying that Dr. Crabb would be different than my experience with that other famous author. When we met, it took about 10 seconds to recognize that he would be. By the time I dropped Dr. Crabb back at the airport the following day, I felt like I was saying goodbye to a dear friend. And yes, his lecture was great, too. He inspired us to think well and carefully about the healing place of the church in contemporary society.

In that first encounter, I learned that Dr. Crabb's character matched the person I knew him to be from his writings, and that consistency blessed me incredibly. I have recommended Dr. Crabb's books to many people since that initial meeting at Wheaton College, and every time I do I mention that Larry Crabb as a person is—as far as I can tell—an exact match to the person I would wish him to be after reading his written words. For a season I tried writing trade books myself, though never with much success. Whenever I wrote a trade book I found myself trying to model the earnest, authentic, open style that I learned from Dr. Crabb and his writing. This, it seems to me, reflects the kingdom of God on earth and all the hope it holds for honest, real people to admit to their struggles and lean into the life-giving grace offered us through Jesus. I have moved away from the Plymouth Brethren assemblies, and Dr. Crabb has as well, but one of the treasured memories I have from that tradition is the weekly breaking-of-the-bread service where we collectively focused on the life, death, and resurrection of Jesus. There is something about focusing so intently on Jesus that makes it difficult to focus overly much on ourselves. I see a relentless Christ-centeredness in Dr. Crabb's work over the years, and I wonder if that may also have come, at least in part, from the influence of his Plymouth Brethren upbringing.

Psychology and the Church

Two additional points of reference – and deep appreciation – should be mentioned. First, I was amid a shift in career direction around the time that Dr. Crabb gave his Scandrette Lecture at Wheaton College. I had been doing psychological evaluations at a local hospital, mostly with depressed adults and adolescents, and one evening as I was leaving the hospital and walking through the parking lot to my car I realized how often I was cutting-and-pasting a particular paragraph in my psychological reports. It was a paragraph about social isolation. Even in the busy western suburbs of Chicago, with people everywhere you look, the patients I was seeing were feeling alone and isolated. I pondered where people can find connection and community in today's society, and the answer was immediately revealed to me as the church. That parking lot epiphany is when I determined to devote the rest of my career to the relationship between psychology and the church.

Around the same time, Dr. Crabb was experiencing what Kanz and Maier call, "a turning point in his thinking and writing" (p. 47), as evidenced by his books *Connecting* (1997) and *The Safest Place on Earth* (1999, since retitled *Becoming a True Spiritual Community*). These books were formative for me as I was trying to find my way forward and consider how psychology and the church can work together. It was also a time when Dr. Crabb endured a substantial amount of criticism from those in the integration movement, of which I am a part. Personally, I didn't find the criticisms fair because they were mostly defensive, based on Dr. Crabb's idea that much healing can be best accomplished by eldering in the context of a safe church community. This made some reactive, as if he were arguing that there is no place for traditional psychotherapy. Ironically, Dr. Crabb mentioned to me in a chance encounter at a professional meeting that he had started a small clinical practice at the same time he was being unfairly criticized for not believing in clinical practice. His argument, as I understand it, is that the church can step up and address many of the needs that Christian counselors see in their practices, and perhaps can even do it even better than what happens in the counseling office. But he was never suggesting there is no place for counselors and psychotherapists. Unlike many of my integrationist peers, I found myself deeply compelled by his perspectives. Twenty years later, I still believe the church holds incredible promise for the healing of broken souls.

Grace

My remaining point of reference is best captured by his lifetime work more than a single title, but I think of *The Pressure's Off* (2002) as iconic of what I perceive to be a lifelong fascination with grace. I sometimes feel that I also have spent my entire adult life staring at grace, trying to understand its nuances, textures, and meanings. After 40 years of staring, I'm still nowhere close to understanding it, but I find great meaning in the process itself. There is nothing I would rather be gazing at than the grace of God mysteriously revealed in Jesus. This is not a cheap grace that fosters antinomianism, nor is it a grace that leaves us on our own after the moment of conversion. No, this is a robust, persistent, sanctifying grace that keeps us growing toward abundant life in Jesus. It calls us into places of suffering and joy, and is accompanied by gratitude and hope. This is the grace I have stared at for several decades now, and though I've not heard Dr. Crabb say so directly, I suspect the same is true of him. As Kanz and Maier put it (p. 52), Crabb writes of, "a restful experience of grace and reliance upon God who is faithful by those who desire God as their supreme passion." And for Dr. Crabb this is not merely an intellectual pursuit, nor is it a strategy to sell books. This is his heart and soul, revealed in the way he lives.

I count it a great privilege to know Dr. Larry Crabb, a man who guided my way as I muddled through graduate school and has encouraged and directed me ever since through his writings and our professional interactions.

GARY W. MOON

SINGING YOUR OWN SONGS IN HARMONY WITH VOICES FROM THE PAST

I must begin with a commendation to both Kanz and Maier. Their essay was built around the clearly articulated goals of providing an overview of the life and writings of Larry Crabb and making a case for him being an exemplar of Christian psychology. They have accomplished these goals and their provision of an annotated bibliography of Crabb's 26-and-counting books, is a gift to the field. Their scholarship and appreciation of Larry Crabb are wonderfully apparent. My first response is, "Thank you."

My second response will take a bit longer.

I've known about the writing of Larry Crabb for more than three decades; and I've had the good fortune of knowing the person the majority of those years. At my first introduction to his ideas, I didn't like them very much and put his books away. And later, my first correspondence with Larry made me so angry I stayed away from him altogether. But he has apologized and all is good now. Perhaps I should explain.

When I began a Ph.D. program in clinical psychology at a school known for the integration of that discipline with Christian thought, there were only three well-known approaches to harmonizing those disciplines: "Levels of Explanation," "Biblical counseling," and the focus of my program, "Integration" (Johnson & Myers, 2010). At that time, I had not realized that these approaches represented responses to what had happened within the discipline of psychology three-quarters of a century earlier. That was when "modern psychology" began to pack its bags to move across campus, leaving its place near the disciplines of philosophy and religion to move closer to its new family, the physical sciences.

But with this transition, modern psychology left behind a focus on invisible things like soul and spirit. It took a while, but there was a response from Christians in the field.

I thought the "integration" approach would save the day. It would be a route for becoming a licensed mental health professional; respected by the American Psychological Association, American Counseling Association and licensure boards; while also allowing a practitioner to be an out-of-the-closet Christian. My fellow students and professors had heard of Larry Crabb, but there was some fear of bringing his books into the classroom or even putting them on your bookshelf. A psychologist writing about basic and effective principles for *Biblical* counseling, might just mess it up for the rest of us. So I diagnosed him as a slightly more appealing version of a nouthetic counselor and mentally wrote out a treatment plan, but stayed away.

Almost a decade later, degree and licensure in hand, with thousands of hours of clinical practice under my belt, I began to look around for someone who knew better approaches for integrating faith and practice than simply basting a secular ham with sacred glaze. I had become much more open to hearing from more explicit integrators, especially if the possessed the humility to admit feeling as if the clients in practice rooms were in need of "professional help." At a personal level, I began to wonder why it was the saints and devotion masters who had written about the ideas that were healing my soul. And why was it not "okay" to bring those ideas into my work with others?

Then one day in the early 1990s, I got the idea to write a letter to fifteen individuals who were known for writing about what I could only think of as "clinical theology." I asked each to join an advisory board for an institute, The Institute of Clinical Theology, that we would form together to look into the situation of modern psychology ignoring contributions from its soul care past. Fourteen of those I wrote, replied, "Yes," to my request. One person said, "No." It was Larry. I think I mentioned that we got off on the wrong foot.

But in the years to come, he more than made up for this initial lapse of judgment, and we have had scores of wonderful conversations. I knew that we were on better ground when he invited me to attend a very special birthday party. I'll not mention his age at the time. At the party, an Elvis impersonator had been hired to entertain the birthday boy, Larry. The impersonator was good, but when he put the microphone in front of Larry's lips, expecting a laugh at his host's expense, the imitator had quite a shock. Larry began to do Elvis much better than the impersonator. In fact, there were moments when he did Elvis better than Elvis. Larry finished the concert while the hired singer sat in Larry's former chair and watched the show, wearing admiration on his face, along with a slightly red glow of embarrassment.

I learned an important lesson that night about Larry, the Christian psychologist. For him to pull off such an unexpected stunt like that took three things: a lot of talent, a lot of moxy, and a keen ear for when there is something good but slightly off key. Those are exactly the three things that have made Larry Crabb an exemplar in the field of Christian psychology: talent, moxy, and an ear for knowing when other voices are not in perfect harmony with the past.

The Importance of Larry Crabb's Voice

Training and Talent—It is difficult to ignore Larry's training and talent. At the very young age of 26, he earned a Ph.D. in clinical psychology from one of the most prestigious academic programs in the country. While I had initially overlooked his contributions for bringing the terms "biblical counseling" to the integration movement, I had only studied *about* a noteworthy empirical psychologist like Ray Cattell. Larry had studied *with* him. No one, I discovered, could accuse Larry of leaning on the Bible because he didn't know enough about the discipline of psychology.

And later, when I had the privilege of working with Larry Crabb and David Benner in founding *The Conversations Journal: A Forum for Authentic Transformation*, I got an up close view of the keen mind, razor sharp insights, and dazzling communication skills of Larry Crabb. The three of us sometimes mused that as a group we had the minimum amount of theological diversity to be truly ecumenical and the maximum amount that was tolerable. While Larry may have been the conservative theological anchor in the room, there was no debating that his intellect soared high.

I also found out at that time that Larry continued to write his books by hand. His word processor had lead on one end, yellow paint in the middle and a rubber delete feature on the other end. Like an artist with canvas and paint, he liked the physical connection to the images he was crafting. And he also seemed to create best with the smell of coffee grounds and the taste of latte. But don't be fooled by the primitive word processor, it was driven by one of the fastest CPU's I've ever witnessed.

Moxy—Moxy is a good description for how Larry operates. There are more descriptive words I could use, but my mother may read this. What else do you call it when a person is willing to use words that *simultaneously* offend psychologists, professional counselors, conservative Christians, liberal Christians and spiritual directors? And what do you call a person who seems nonplussed by the importance of both licensure and ordination? Or a Reformed thinker who was dismissed from a Reformed seminary ironically named "Grace," for showing too much kindness to thinkers like Freud? Especially if that person's livelihood depends on, to a large extent, having psychologists, counselors, conservative Christians, and spiritual directors buy and recommend his books. I'd still have to go with "moxy." But there may be a better descriptor. Larry is a natural reformer.

Statistically speaking, it seems that God has deemed it important to sprinkle in a few reformers, like yeast, into the dough of his creation. Reformers do not have an easy life. Often, they feel very alone. These are the individuals who are not confined by the normal boundaries that keep others fenced into the pastures of academic disciplines or religious denominations. These are the rare people who dive so deep into the domains of knowledge that they get beneath the demarcations in their search for truth. And when they find it, they come back to the surface to share it with the rest of us. Many see the discoveries of these reformers as threats to their kingdoms. Others experience deep appreciation and set out to live their lives in a radically different way because of what has been offered. Larry is one of those people who dives deeply and is willing to speak the words that have been found there. That takes a lot of moxy.

Harmony with Voices from the Past— Reformers who have an impact that jumps across generations have a keen ear for both cacophony and symphony. They know when notes are off. They know when they blend to produce something much more than a sum of the parts. In personal correspondence with Kanz (2015), Larry wrote these words concerning his early days as a practitioner of modern clinical psychology: "...What professionals called 'psychotherapy' could better be understood as passionate, wisdom-based conversations." And as Kanz and Maier offer, this understanding has persisted in Larry's writing and thinking.

Larry has followed his own words in a search for wisdom-based answers for life's problems and pain, especially in the area of relationships. During his career he has followed that path from modern psychology through the pages of Scripture and back to the ancient domain of spiritual formation and direction. While not dismissing wisdom from modern psychology, he has heard and harmonized with voices from other disciplines and across the ages.

Willard and Crabb

One of the reasons I like the thought and work of Larry Crabb so much is because there are so many places where his contributions harmonize with another person who worked to provide a truly Christian psychology, Dallas Willard. Like Dallas, Larry also: 1) is highly trained in one academic discipline, but better known for writing in another; 2) has a high view of Scripture and peppers most published paragraphs with Biblical references; 3) is very familiar with personal pain; 4) looks to the past while writing to modern audiences; 5) is driven to find wise answers to the most foundational questions concerning how to live well; 6) sees the church as a living laboratory for learning how to live well; 7) has spent a career waging war against the ideas of modernism; and 8) stayed grounded by a few driving and consistent concerns.

I did not mention that each is known for a marvelous baritone voice, but I will focus below on four of the key ideas that, in my opinion, unite the work of Dallas Willard and Larry Crabb and lay a solid foundation for a truly Christian psychology.

Robust Metaphysical Realism: Invisible Things are also Real

As Kanz and Maier observe, understanding and interacting with the Trinity is very important to the work of Larry Crabb. He sees the word "perichoresis," or the Trinity's ongoing dance of other-centered love, as being a model for human relationships with each other and with God and as something that actually exists. Foundational to the thought of Dallas Willard is a belief in a robust metaphysical realism (Willard, 1997). Both believe that invisible things like the Trinity and the Kingdom of God are part of reality as much and more so than are lab rats, salivating dogs and even electrochemical reactions in the brain.

Epistemic Realism: It is Possible to Learn from and Interact with Invisible Reality

While Willard's work in the area of epistemic realism is more obvious and is meticulously conveyed in his books, *The Spirit of the Disciplines: Understanding how*

God Changes Lives (Willard, 1988), and *Hearing God: Developing a Conversational Relationship with God* (Willard, 1984/2012), Crabb's belief in the ability to interact with and draw knowledge from invisible reality, and his willingness to write about this is remarkable. His book *66 Love Letters* (Crabb, 2009a) is, quite literally, a running conversation between Larry and the Divine, which also invites the reader into the story of God. At the heart of so much of the writings of both Willard and Crabb is the belief that the pathway to true happiness and blessing is found in living life in a restored relationship *with* the living and communicating Trinity and that our best opportunity for putting the good news of Jesus into practice (living interactively with the Trinity here and now) is found in our current relationships.

Christian Anthropology: We are Designed for Just Such Interaction

Both Crabb (1987) and Willard (2002) like to teach about the person using models of concentric circles. While the number of circles drawn may have been different, both used such flat maps to convey aspects of the person that would be included in modern psychology: cognitive, physical/behavioral, and affective/emotional, as well as the aspect of volition. They both described the interactive nature of these aspects as well as the importance of the unconscious mind. But more importantly to the development of a Christian psychology, both Crabb and Willard believed in the importance of aspects of the person *largely ignored* by modern psychology; invisible, immeasurable aspects of the person such as soul, spirit, and the deepest longings of the heart.

Knowledge Produces Authentic Transformation

As Kanz and Maier underscore, Crabb's primary motivation for writing *Effective Biblical Counseling* (Crabb, 1977) was his determination to "understand a biblical theology of how change occurs." And he came to view the primary goal of Christian living as a growth in maturity, which involves immediate obedience to God and long-range growth of character.

Like Crabb, Willard also believed that obedience is the "engine" that pulls the train of transformation and maturity of character. He believed that authentic transformation happens in the normal events of life as we center our minds on Christ, yield to the actions of the Holy Spirit, and take on new habits of character through planned and practiced spiritual disciplines. That is, to be living in an eternal sort of way through the experience of a transforming friendship with the Trinity, which comes by *knowing* God (John 17:3). If the knowing is real, it should produce real and measurable change within the individual (Willard, 2009).

Real and measurable change; now this is a desirable outcome on which both Christian psychology and modern psychology can agree.

Summary

This has been a remarkably positive critique. I believe that it is deserved. If pressed, I could and have (in conversation with Larry) offered a few ideas for things that could be improved upon. It is my subjective opinion that Larry underestimates the importance of his own training in modern psychology as well as the importance of his own intuitive skills in teaching others his approach to counseling and spiritual direction. I believe to most effectively teach others the insights and experiential skills he offers would require years of systematic study as opposed to a single class or retreat.

And speaking of "spiritual direction," I wish Larry would call his training schools by a different name, not because what is taught is not in that broad domain but because it is so different from what is usually associated with spiritual direction. Larry offers remarkable "schools of biblical and relational wisdom," which draw from the domains of Christian psychology, biblical counseling, and historic models of soul care. That is a mouthful, but I do believe different nomenclature would help to clarify any potential confusion with the current climate of spiritual direction training.

And, if I'm being completely honest, I wish Crabb were 50% more excited about classical spiritual exercises and 50% less excited about Reformed theology. I have tried and failed to get him more on board by pointing out that Jesus was a frequent participant in spiritual disciplines. And I've tried to at least plant the seed in Larry's mind that it is unlikely that Jesus would adopt a plan for withholding his best thinking for 1,500 years before releasing it.

But that is the 1%. The 99% is that I believe Crabb is an exemplar of Christian psychology and I applaud and affirm that his foundations for writing are also crucial pillars to a Christian approach to psychology: obedience to Christ, perichoretic life *with* the Trinity, understanding and following the deepest desires of one's heart, which flow from the Spirit, learning to mortify the "flesh" (our self-reliance, not body) while vivifying the spirit, including Biblical truth and wisdom as anchor points for understanding the person and pathway to deep happiness, and the importance of diving deeply enough to find unifying truth.

JAMIE RASMUSSEN

EMBRACING THIRST

This rather brief, albeit encompassing, overview of Larry Crabb's life work could alternatively be titled, "The Transformation of Larry Crabb." Many people grow over time in their chosen professions, but few undergo what popular culture calls an "extreme makeover." However, when one departs from conventional norms within his or her profession, and does so with significant and positive impact, this is transformational. This is precisely what Larry Crabb has accomplished.

Right around the time that Crabb was finishing his sixth book, *Hope When You're Hurting*, co-authored with Dan Allender (1985), I was writing my undergraduate senior thesis on the work of Jay Adams. In the process of my research, I was exposed to many of the early pioneers of what would become a Christian approach to psychology. Narramore, Solomon, Collins, Dobson and others were the academicians and practitioners who shaped much of the early focus for Christians desiring to utilize the findings of psychology in their biblical worldview. Following either a cognitive behavioral model (utilizing thoughts derived from a biblical understanding) or a behavior modification model (utilizing behavior patterns found in the Bible), much of the early integrationist work was focused on an attempt to fit the prevailing psychology models into a biblical framework. For myself as a young psychology major with aspirations to serve God and help others, this was quite an exciting time.

When I was halfway through my seminary education, I read my first book by Larry Crabb, *Inside Out* (1988/2007/2013). It was transformative for me both professionally and personally. Professionally, I was exposed to ideas that combined rich psychological insights with cogent biblical exegesis. In *Inside Out*, psychology and theology didn't seem forced together, but rather an organic infusion of two worlds with which I was rather familiar. My worldview was on the cusp of a sizable paradigm shift. Personally, I was shaken. I found myself exposed and understood in a way I had not experienced up to that point in my life. I was the one digging "broken cisterns" in many wrong places.

Over the years, as I have read Crabb's books and interacted with him on a personal level, I have identified no less than three broad constructs that I believe are core to the transformative nature of Crabb's life work. They have also been integral to my professional and personal development. Each of these themes are mentioned in the target article by Kanz and Maier, yet I want to underline and affirm them. These three themes are, for me, the essence of why Crabb's writings and teaching are so critical for generations to come.

First is Crabb's insistence on both a *biblical* and *relational* framework in understanding God and people. His perspective affects how we view sin, salvation and sanctification. Crabb refuses to allow sin to reside solely in behavioral and cognitive realms. He challenges his readers to view sin as primarily a *relational* entity. When we were once discussing a popular Christian author's view of sin, Crabb commented, "I don't think this person's hamartiology goes deep enough." He meant that limiting sin to one's behaviors and thoughts is not giving God's revelation its due emphasis. Sin is ultimately rooted in how one relates. Sin is seen in the fullness of thoughts, emotions and will as they express themselves toward God and others. Jesus taught this: "There is nothing outside a person that by going into him can defile him, but the things that come out of a person are what defile him" (Mark 7:15, English Standard Version). Conversely, salvation and sanctification also are measured relationally. As Crabb puts it in his recent book, *A Different Kind of Happiness* (2016), "Bringing God's *relational* Kingdom to earth by becoming increasingly *relationally* holy – by Christians learning to put Christ's way of relating on display first to each other and then overflowing with Jesus-like love to the world" (emphasis mine) It is relationship that God is seeking in our lives. Relationship--which the Bible affirms--is core to our understanding of the Fall, redemption, and what it means to live a life set apart for

God. In my assessment, Larry Crabb has laid this out in a biblical fashion that transcends most of what has been written since the genesis of an integrationist approach to theology and psychology. I would be remiss in failing to mention Crabb's emphasis on Trinitarian theology. In his regularly held week-long School of Spiritual Direction, he talks about the "dance of the Trinity;" the eternal, mutually satisfying relationality which the three Persons of the Trinity share. Crabb points out that if we were to ask what the Trinity has done for all eternity, even before the creation of the world, the answer is that they have been involved in *relationship*--God-glorifying, other-centered, joy-producing relationship. This "dance" is a pattern God has given us as to what he likewise values in his creation. Though plenty of scholars and authors have written on the Trinity down through the centuries, Crabb has integrated this understanding of God richly into how we, as his children, should relate. This idea of Trinitarian relating has affected my church to the point that our elders and staff have incorporated formal times of "soul care" with each other into our roles as pastors and elders.

The second major construct I believe Crabb has uniquely erected is his determination to see spiritual and psychological formation occur at the local level. Though Crabb has great respect for pastors and professional counselors, he has made it clear that a biblical pattern must follow what the Reformers called the "priesthood of all believers" (1 Peter 2:5). This is obviously a major departure from the assumed norms of nearly all of the early integrationists. The discipline of psychology is firmly built upon a position in which professional experts are the primary people helpers. In many pastoral circles, the same view is found. Born once again from a biblical conviction, Crabb made the bold move early on in his thinking to argue that believers who learn to listen to the Spirit at rich and deep levels can be primary agents of help and healing. He believes this so deeply that he shuns most titles that professionals use. He asks everyone to call him "Larry." When we were once spending a day together in Denver, I commented to him how much I appreciate him "mentoring" me. He got a confused look on his face and said, "I don't see it that way. What I see is two thirsty men meeting together for the day and having a Spirit-led conversation." This view is transformative. It gives the Church great hope that local, lay-led spiritual formation can be the seedbed of growth and change. It fulfills much of what the New Testament envisions as the Church becomes the literal "body of Christ" (1 Corinthians 12:27).

The third and most significant broad construct from my perspective is Crabb's portrayal of "thirst" as central to our spiritual experience. For the first twenty years in my walk with God (I did not come to faith until early adulthood), I was chronically dissatisfied in my experience of God. Even as a pastor leading the charge in local church settings, I felt spiritually impotent at times. Like many pastors, I presented a strong and unified front as I preached the Word, counseled people, and performed my pastoral duties. Within my interior life, however, I felt consistently inadequate and lacking in my experience of the spiritual reality I talked boldly about. One day, as I was unloading this verbally on Larry, he asked me, "Are you thirsty? Do you have burning desire for more of God? Is there a gnawing in your spirit that longs for more of him?" I responded, "Of course! That's the point. I have had this since the day I bent the knee to him and gave my life to him." He then said to me, "Have you ever considered that the thirst is a great part of the experience? Has it ever occurred to you that the longing is part and parcel of what it means to be his follower this side of heaven?" This affected me deeply. "As the deer pants for the water brooks, so my soul pants for You, O God" (Psalm 42:1, New American Standard Bible).

We live in a day and age where there are many varieties of Christian experience: charismatic expressions, liturgy, hymnody, modern praise music, Bible study, missions, service, and prayer – the list is lengthy and full. These may deliver profound experiences of healing, purpose, wholeness, and joy for some people, yet none of them alone seem to promise a universal experience for all. What Crabb has put forth is something that every single follower of Jesus can relate to: thirst. We are all thirsty. We all have deep-seated longings and desires for more of God. And it seems to get more intense the closer we get to heaven. Once I began embracing my thirst, even parking in front of it and not doing a shameful drive-by, I have found it a wonderful experience in drawing me closer to the Lord.

Any cursory reading of Larry Crabb's writings reveals that he lives an honest, intellectually curious, spiritually attuned life. He also lives a disturbed life. He wrestles with vexing spiritual and psychological issues for which there are no easy answers. He does this by examining not only other's souls, but his own as well. He has uniquely responded to this with a level of biblical and relational understanding that stands out among the crowd. I believe his writings and influence will last for generations to come.

SIANG-YANG TAN

A CHRISTIAN PSYCHOLOGY RESPONSE

Kanz and Maier have written a very clear, concise and yet comprehensive essay on the Christian psychology of Larry Crabb, a well-known and widely read Christian psychologist. It covers all of his 26 published books, from Crabb on *Basic Principles of Biblical Counseling* (1975) and *Effective Biblical Counseling* (1977) to *When God's Ways Make No Sense* (2018), his most recent book. Crabb is now in his 70s, and his books span over four decades of substantial, biblical reflection on a variety of significant topics, most of which are relevant to Christian psychology. Kanz and Maier have provided very helpful and succinct summaries of each of Crabb's books. They have also highlighted six major themes from his books: model building, the role of the church, gender, suffering, the Trinity, and the new covenant.

Crabb's published books reflect the development and maturing of his thoughts and ideas over the four decades of time from the 1970s to today. He has always been a creative, original, brilliant, and biblical thinker and writer. Kanz and Maier concluded that the majority of his books have shown a lifelong commitment to Christian psychology and more importantly to me, his deep commitment to the Triune God through Jesus Christ as his Lord and Savior, and to inspired Scripture as God's eternal Word. Their hope is that future generations of Christians, church leaders, and Christian psychologists will read Crabb's books and benefit from hearing his message for the world and for the church in as clear and consistent a way as possible.

I personally have been blessed by Crabb's writings and books over these four decades, which have also influenced me and helped shape my thinking and writing as a Christian psychologist, especially in my work on the integration of psychology and Christian faith, lay counseling, Christian counseling and therapy, and Christian psychology. I have known Larry Crabb as a personal friend for many years now, and we have kept in touch over the years by telephone as well as in personal meetings, usually at conferences where we have served as speakers or presenters. I keep him and his wonderful wife Rachael, and their family daily in prayer. I deeply appreciate him and his significant writings and books, as well as presentations at many Christian counseling and pastors' conferences. He is truly a deep and mature Christian man, committed to God and a biblical, Christian perspective on life, including counseling and spiritual direction and formation. Yet, he is very vulnerable and authentic in his talks as well as in his books, touching and connecting with the people who hear and/or read him. While I very much appreciate the excellent summary by Kanz and Maier on the Christian psychology of Larry Crabb and his career on the road less travelled and his faithfulness to Christ all these decades, I have several other comments in response to their essay that I trust will provide a fuller Christian psychology perspective.

First, Crabb made substantial contributions to the development and training of Christian lay counselors, especially in his earlier writings (e.g., Crabb, 1975, 1977, 1987), and training seminars on biblical counseling through his former Institute of Biblical Counseling before he founded NewWay Ministries with his later focus on spiritual direction and connecting with deeper-level soul talk (Crabb, 1997, 1994, 2003). Lay counseling is a crucial, biblically based ministry (see Tan & Scalise, 2016) and Kanz and Maier could have highlighted more Crabb's significant contributions to this area of lay counseling. Christian psychology (see Johnson, 2007, 2017) will focus on the ministry of caring and counseling in the church, including lay counseling, in addition to other professional and scientific areas of psychology.

Second, Crabb's major contributions have been in model building and his biblical reflections on topics such as the role of the church, gender, suffering, the Trinity and the new covenant: in other words, more in the areas of theory/theology and practice, and almost none in the area of empirical research. Of course, one person cannot do or cover everything! However, empirical research is a central part of contemporary psychology, as well as of Christian psychology that takes seriously academic and scientific psychology as a field. There are other Christian psychologists who are very involved in conducting empirical research in a number of significant areas of psychology, including Christian counseling and psychotherapy (e.g., see Tan 2011a; Worthington, Johnson, Hook & Aten, 2013).

Third, while Crabb has shared original and biblical reflections (e.g., see Crabb, 2009a) that are theologically sound, more of historical theology, as well as biblical theology and systematic theology can be fruitfully used in his future writings. A specific area that can be more fully explored and mined is the wisdom of the Patristic period, and the care of souls in the classic tradition with the early church fathers and mothers (e.g., see Oden, 1984, 1992; Knabb, 2016, 2017; Knabb & Frederick, 2017; see also Johnson, 2007, 2017). In particular, Knabb (2016, 2017) who is a Christian psychologist and on the faculty at California Baptist University, has made some recent significant contributions to integrating the contemplative traditions and practices of the early desert Christians and biblical perspectives with Acceptance and Commitment Therapy (ACT), a leading mindfulness-based cognitive-behavioral therapy (see Tan, 2011b; Rosales & Tan, 2016). He has also developed and described an eight-week contemplative prayer program for helping Christians with chronic worry (Knabb & Frederick, 2017), with some preliminary empirical support for its effectiveness (Knabb, Frederick, & Cumming III, 2017).

Fourth and finally, while Crabb has made substantial contributions to model building in the integration of psychology and the Christian faith, and to Christian psychology, he has not written a larger and more comprehensive systematic overview of the field of counseling and psychotherapy from a distinctively Christian or biblical perspective as have Jones and Butman (2011) and Tan (2011a). Christian psychology will need more efforts in this area, especially in developing Christian approaches to specific schools of counseling and psychotherapy (see Johnson & Hardin, 2014), as well as focusing on the unique therapeutic resources of the Christian faith as Johnson (2017) has recently done. To be fair, however, Crabb's (1975, 1977) earlier work on effective biblical counseling was basically a Christian approach to Cognitive Behavioral Therapy (CBT).

In conclusion, Larry Crabb is definitely an outstanding pioneer in the field of Christian counseling and psychotherapy, as well as in Christian psychology. We all owe him a great debt and heartfelt appreciation for his inspiring and life-transforming substantial contributions and writings. Thank God for Larry Crabb, and to God be the glory!

BRETT VADEN

WALKING THE HARD AND EASY ROAD

K anz and Maier claim that Crabb's approach to psychology and counseling "captures the heart of Johnson's proposal." Johnson (2007) himself identifies Crabb as a Christian psychologist. Are they right? Do Crabb's works exemplify what it means to do the work of Christian psychology? I think so, though with a small caveat. In this commentary, I want to add to what Kanz and Maier have written by identifying an important and beneficial dichotomy Crabb offers us. This dichotomy, which is really a pair of complements, naturally derives out of Crabb's core theological convictions, which are rooted in and ruled by the Bible. But before considering Crabb's foundational beliefs and the pair of complements that may constitute his weightiest contribution, let me offer my caveat.

Caveat: We Need Both Prongs

In his proposal for Christian psychology, Johnson has called for a two-pronged strategy: first, Christian psychologists need to work for the Christian community, seeking to "publish in Christian publishing organs, interact with fellow Christians in psychology conferences and seek to minister to Christians in soul care and to influence non-Christians to consider the claims of Christ" (Johnson, 2007, p. 255). Second, we need to enter the broader sphere of psychology in the world and help to fashion a "pluralistic psychology." This second prong especially includes tasks related to empirical scientific research (e.g., designing psychological measures, discovering statistically meaningful findings) in an effort to collaborate with non-Christian theorists and practitioners in building up the wider community of research and practice.

In his efforts to address topics like community and soul care, Crabb has focused mainly on the first prong, that is, addressing the spiritual, psychological, and relational problems of people familiar with or already belonging to the Christian community. While no doubt his works have touched many others outside the church, he has not devoted his most direct attention to helping construct a "pluralistic psychology." In looking to Crabb's contributions, therefore, readers should not expect a robust engagement with other thinkers outside Christianity. This fact does nothing to minimize the value of his works, for they provide a rich (and still-growing) corpus of wisdom and knowledge. Indeed, while Crabb may not exemplify what it means to do

Christian psychology on the more pluralistic and scientific level of empirical research and translation of other texts and theories, he succeeds remarkably on the *sapiential* level of spiritual direction. Thus, the caveat: Crabb's works provide a body of spiritual wisdom, and in that respect he captures the most important level of Johnson's proposal (i.e., "the heart" of it), though not all of it. I only mention this caveat to point out that we need both prongs in order to adequately pursue our work in the church and the world.

Crabb's Core Convictions

When one looks at the philosophical underpinnings of Crabb's thinking, it is apparent that he would agree with Johnson that "a distinctly Christian *version* of psychology . . . . flows from a Christian understanding of human nature and therefore can be distinguished from alternative versions of psychology based on different world views" (Johnson, 2007, p. 9). For example, Crabb asserts, "Psychology apart from God can never provide a meaningful framework for movement in the counseling office" (1975, p. 24). In *Basic Principles of Biblical Counseling* (1975), Crabb offers us a window into the formative process that directed him to differentiate between a secular and Christian view of psychology:

As I restudied what I had learned in graduate school, it became clearly and frighteningly apparent that most of what I was believing and doing as a professional psychologist was built upon the swaying foundation of humanism, a fervent belief in the self-sufficiency of man. As a Christian committed to a biblical view of man, I could not make the psychological thinking in which I had been trained dovetail with basic biblical beliefs like the fall of man, his separation from God, his desperate need of divine assistance, the promises of love, joy and peace to those who accepted the free gift of eternal life through Jesus' substitutionary death and who learned to live in the power of the Holy Spirit" (p. 11).

In contrast to a psychology built on "the self-sufficiency of man"—or, in Johnson's terms, the individual "autonomous Self"—a Christian framework took control early in Crabb's approach to psychology, and one of the results has been a focus on the dynamic of spiritual community.

A Pair of Complements: Crabb's Weightiest Contribution?

Throughout his books, one of the most important themes Crabb weaves is that of relationship, or community. At the foundation of the Christian life is one's relationship with God, on which other relationships are securely based. Without God, basic needs like believing oneself worthwhile and having significance and security cannot be satisfied. This fact is crucial: "Biblical counselors must be able to intelligently assert and defend the proposition that Christ really is the necessary and sufficient answer for the needs of people. Otherwise they may come across as blindly dogmatic and unconvincing" (Crabb, 1975, p. 56). When conformity to Christ and God's glory are understood as the fundamental requirement and context for living, says Crabb, "Now each moment of life . . . . can be seen as part of a larger meaningful whole" (p. 58). So monolithic is this dependence on God that "I literally need nothing other than what God allows me to have" (p. 66).

Yet, God's centrality in our lives by no means denigrates "the importance and desirability of human relationships" (Crabb, 1975, p. 70), because God has created us not only to need him, but to often need him through experiencing relationships with other people. Our desire for God is concurrent with a desire for spiritual community: "'It's the Lord I want...' That cry from your heart is your longing to be part of a true church, to participate in spiritual community, to engage in spiritual conversations of worship with God and of co-journeying with others" (Crabb, 1999, p. 19). Instead of relying on "SelfTalk" to heal ourselves, an overarching goal in life should be "to discover my desire for God and indulge that passion with all my soul . . . . You can do that for me. And I can do it for you . . . . We can learn to talk with each other in ways that arouse our passion for God" (Crabb, 2003, pp. 8-9). In God's plan to satisfy our basic needs, Crabb says "the local Christian community is God's primary instrument" (1999, p. 74). In light of this fact and also owing to the fallen nature and common deficiencies of these communities, Crabb says the "resources of the local church" need to be improved (1975, p. 75). Indeed, his career has constituted a long and sustained effort to accomplish this task of helping people "connect" in the context of the local church, which ideally is "the safest place on earth" (Crabb, 1999).

How has Crabb gone about this task? In two ways: one that feels harder—i.e., calling people to love better through suffering, as Jesus loved—and one that feels easier—i.e., welcoming people into the freedom to be authentic in their brokenness and to experience grace. These two ways form a pair of complements that may constitute Crabb's weightiest contribution.

The first and difficult way that Crabb has spoken to us is seen in statements like the following: "For God's sake, don't expect it to be easy"; "It's not easy, but it's worth it" (Crabb, 1999, p. 3; 11). And, from his recent book, *A Different Kind of Happiness* (2016): "The happiness of Jesus can be ours if we fight the battle to love, a battle that can be won, never fully till heaven but substantially now, only on the narrow road" (Crabb, 2016, p. 42). For Crabb, there is just one path to the good life, and it is found only in Jesus Christ, through confession, repentance, and trust in Christ's atonement for us (1975). The deepest problem humans face is their separation from God, and until they experience restoration with Him, small temporal problems may be solved in life by "approximating biblical principles," but people will not have a truly good life now nor in eternity (Crabb, 1975, p. 17). While God created us with needs to be satisfied, our felt needs should be subordinated to faith and obedience: "I reject a need-centered, anthropocentric understanding of human nature. I do not believe (and never have) that anyone should devote himself or herself to gaining a sense of personal security and significance before they get around to obeying God and loving others" (Crabb, 1999, p. 7). Recognizing our penchant for wrongly prioritizing and ordering our loves, Crabb has subversively exposed that tendency and declaimed it. Echoing C. S. Lewis, who said, "Put first things first and second things are thrown in" (2007, p. 111), Crabb exhorts us to talk in ways that catch each other up into "another sphere, the world of the Spirit, where *first things are first and second things are second*" (1999, p. xiii, emphasis mine). His recent book, *A Different Kind of Happiness* (2016), is focused sharply on clarifying the hard and narrow side of Christianity by arguing that true joy, or "first thing happiness," goes hand in hand with loving others in an outward, relational way like God does, and does not depend on blessings or the felt presence of God. Learning to love like Jesus is the only "real and sustaining joy" and "only a few even find the road that leads to life, and fewer remain on it while the forming process unfolds" (Crabb, 2016, p. 48). Conscious of his career-long emphasis on the narrow road and the darker side of the Christian life, Crabb explains that in doing so he has wanted to distance himself from promoting "second thing happiness," which, though nice to experience and often filled with blessings, "can erode the desire to pay whatever price is required to know God so well that we discover first thing happiness, the true joy that develops only as we love like Jesus" (2016, p. 38). A practical application involves prayer: we should seek to pray the kinds of prayers that Jesus always answers. Such prayers do not ask for blessings to make life pleasant, nor simply "if it be your will" prayers that hope for ease but submit to difficulty, but the hardest kind of prayer that asks

God, "Make me like Jesus, a little Christ who puts Him on display by how I relate" (Crabb, 2016, p. 78). Though seemingly innocuous, such a prayer is another way of asking for a life conformed to Christ, who loved perfectly and submitted himself entirely to God's will, even to the point of taking up his cross. In this respect, Crabb's approach to soul care may feel not only intimidating to us, but (seemingly) soul-crushing!

On the other hand, Crabb has consistently upheld the truth that God intends to satisfy our deepest longings *through* his grace and *in* eternity, not through human merit in the present. In *The Pressure's Off: There's a New Way to Live* (2002), Crabb exposes the false belief that happiness and well-being come through obeying the "Law of Linearity," which has us doing A to experience B, yet leads us away from God. Living as a Christian is not about fully achieving all God's blessings now, but about experiencing the New Life in which "the pressure's off" of us to win our way to happiness: "The spiritual journey is *not* about living as we should so life works as we want. It's *not* a linear path" (Crabb, 2002, p. 26). Rather, the Christian life it is "rooted in liberty, the freedom of grace: Come as you are, trembling, and learn to rest. Then go out into life doing what's right because you're privileged to do so, because you want to be holy, not because doing right is the way to a pleasant life" (Crabb, 2002, p. 26). Although some degree of suffering is an inherent part of this journey, so is joyful communion with God: "We cannot count on God to protect us from suffering of any kind or measure. The worst evil can happen to the best Christian. But we can count on God to enable us to draw near to Him whatever happens and, eventually, to experience deep joy when we do" (Crabb, 2002, p. 195). Using a personal illustration (which Crabb does often) from his childhood, he describes how, instead of pining for God to unlock the door and let us out to play, what we need is to be with Him—sometimes in the dark and in suffering—until He opens the door to eternity. Elsewhere he writes, "Life is all about knowing God! It's all about him, and because he loves us, it's all about him and me, him and you, you and me in him. Knowing him is what I want more than anything. And knowing the Father is what Jesus makes possible for me!" (Crabb, 2003, p. 7-8). In sum, the relieving truth that Crabb proclaims about Christianity is that, because of Christ, we can present ourselves authentically to God apart from our merits and without fear for our sin, and that when we do he cultivates true joy in us, which is knowing him.

Conclusion

Kanz and Meier have done a solid service by calling us to attend to the works of Larry Crabb. Indeed, as they have stated, what he has given "the church and the world still needs to be heard, as consistently and clearly as ever." I will never forget reading his book *Real Church: Does it Exist? Can I Find It?* (2009b), not only because he helped me articulate the disillusionment and desires that I was feeling at that time towards the church, but because he modeled a way for me to earnestly and authentically deal with my unmet needs before God, and in a way that resulted most of all in my own repentance and striving to love better, rather than in shoring up my grievances against others. And that lesson is, I think, what we most need to learn from him: how to experience the grace-filled "pressure's off" life of living *coram deo* and thereby be changed from "the inside out."

ED WELCH

REFLECTIONS ON A GROWING SAINT WHO FINDS REST IN JESUS

Thank you for the privilege to consider this wholesale review of Larry's books and to respond publicly to it. It has been a treat to think about his contributions. I confess that I have not read all of Larry's books. I am reading *66 Love Letters* (2009a) and I have not gotten to *Real Church* (2009b) in detail, but I have read most of his books, am familiar with the broad strokes of his ministry, and have also been able to hear him speak a number of times. Here are a few thoughts.

Growth and Humility

I have always appreciated how Larry is spiritually on the move. He is, indeed, an intense and passionate man, with a hint of restlessness. Yet this movement reveals his theology. Larry always wants to be growing. Though sanctified and washed through Jesus, the outworkings of that definitive act are worked out over the course of our lives—Larry has taken this to heart. Larry is always growing, always wanting more of Christ, always listening. If he were not growing, he would stop writing. This alone makes his contribution necessary and valuable.

I think Larry's distinctive voice emerged in *The Marriage Builder* (1982/1992/2013), and it came with this commitment to humility and growth. In it was an implicit pact: "What I am about to say must first touch my own soul before I can try to touch your own. Anything else would be audacious and wrong. So bear with me as I work through these matters alongside you." These are my own words but I suspect he would acknowledge the essence of them.

His theological movement here is evident. He was persuaded that the personal God *engages*, is moved by, and responds to his people. We, in turn, respond to him and speak from our hearts to him, and since this style is fundamental to the kingdom of God, we do it with each other. Jesus Christ has made the way for this fellowship and communion, and we will have all eternity to practice it.

His spiritual movement was apparent in other books too. He has, I think, moved from early books on counseling methods and discerning complex motivations toward knowing Christ and pursuing communion with him. In this, he has not distanced himself from his earlier work, but he has worked to have it all settle more explicitly on the person of Jesus. This movement has even impacted his professional identity. Whereas he began as a self-identified Christian psychologist, he later identified more as a spiritual director and friend.

I suggest that there is also movement from *Safest Place on Earth* (1999) and *Soul Talk* (2003) to *66 Love Letters* (2009a). Authentic community can be invigorating. We all would like to be known, or at least have someone try to know us. But skillful sharing and knowing can never be an end in itself. *66 Love Letters* anchors our mutual care in the Spirit working through Scripture.

Simplicity

Larry's interest in model building was apparent in his first book and continues to his last. This too reveals something about him. He has a mind that values coherence and clarity, a whole rather than pieces. Yet, here again, his theology wins the day. He believes that God himself is one God, coherent and consistent within himself. As such, his revelation will be united and systematic. And this revelation is available to all God's people so it should be simple.

What makes model building a challenge is that Scripture doesn't present counseling models in the way we might prefer. Instead, we watch people and we watch God through stories. We participate in corporate praise, consternation and lament. We are led through different genres of wisdom literature. And all of it resides in a cultural context that is very different from our own.

Aware of this, Larry has aimed for a course that recognizes that Scripture and people are complex, deep and full of mysteries while at the same time Scripture's meaning is available to us all, especially now that we live in the new covenant. His job, therefore, has been to present his understanding of Scripture in a way that is vivid, usable, helpful and balanced. That is, he has aimed to draw from Scripture a working model for soul care.

More to Come

Larry, no doubt, has projects in motion and ideas galore that would both surprise us and be consistent with the trajectory of his work.

Notice how he wants to hear the voice of God even more. (The way to hear the voice of God, he says, is to capture the message of every book in Scripture and then explore the details).

Notice his interest in the church, growing in faith, openness, and inter-dependence as the grandest defense of the gospel to a needy and broken world.

Notice his Apostle John-like interest in the call to know the Lover, be known by the Lover, and love others deeply.

Larry has invited us to walk with him, and his hope is that we would realize the potential of new life in the age of the Spirit. Don't expect him to double back and walk us through the details of one-hour-per-week professional counseling sessions. Instead, expect him to take us through the sins and sufferings of life on to the enjoyment of being in Christ.

And a More Personal Response

Larry and I come from the same era—we followed soon after pioneers such as Adams, Narramore, Collins, and others who wanted to bring Scripture to counseling. We both had graduate training in secular psychology and practiced as psychologists. I suspect my pre-graduate school seminary training caused me to emphasize, even during my graduate work, the religious nature of psychotherapy and how it could be conceived of as a secular version of pastoral care, but Larry's take on secular psychotherapy has always been very similar to my own. (To use his different categories, I have thought of myself, and biblical counseling as a whole, as Egyptian spoilers more than nothing-buttery).

Most importantly, we share the same fascination, which is to draw out from the treasure chest of Scripture realities that surprise and the Person who changes everything. And while we aim for simplicity, we loathe the simplistic or trite because it is so out of synch with God's communication to us and the complexity of creation.

I wrote one article (Welch, 1994) that briefly discussed *Understanding People* (1987/2013). At the time I thought of him as an in-house colleague because we both desired to draw our counseling model out of Scripture, but I am certain that I would write that article differently today (I share his interest in growth and change). At least, I would have wanted to get his feedback before it was published. It was around that time that I had begun to feel the sting of being misunderstood, and I hoped to write about other writers in a way that they would feel understood. If I remember correctly, the article touched on Larry's work on certain human needs and suggested that these needs (for significance, in particular) were best further examined for their idolatrous tendencies rather than simply assumed. What I left implicit was that our core agenda—to draw out a model of care and counsel from Scripture—is identical. That is too important to be left implicit.

One final point. Among the many details that I share with Larry is his insistence that we live in an intensely personal world in which we are responsively engaged with the triune God and other people. As a result, God and others are always leaving their mark on us, at least that is our hope. With this in mind, I would not want to move on to other projects until I identify how Larry, through Jason and Bryan's article, has changed me.

66 Love Letters (2009a) is the one that stands out at this moment. As the essay by Kanz and Maier indicates, it is a kind of magnum opus. I think I understand clearly why Larry persevered in this project, and I take some pleasure in knowing his purposes, but I have so appreciated the actual letters themselves. I have been doing my own version of this project for a number of years, and Larry has shown me how to do it much better. Even more, the letters, though Larry's words, have been a more articulate voice for my own soul, and, for that alone, I am in his debt.

Many blessings on his life and future ministry.

KEP CRABB

A SON'S RESPONSE

It's a beautiful Monday night in Colorado as I begin to organize my thoughts for this article on Larry Crabb. Let me introduce myself. I'm Kep Crabb, the oldest son of Larry and Rachael Crabb. Being Larry's son, I think it's safe to say that he has impacted me in ways different from any of the other contributors to this book. Over my 49 years of life, I've often been asked, "What's it like having Dr. Larry Crabb as your father?" I usually just reply, "He's the only father I've ever known," realizing that if I were to thoughtfully answer that question, we would be there all day. But now, as I sit and reflect on his life, and my life with him, I see how he has provided a glimpse of Jesus and when you are with him, you realize you're with someone who really cares.

As I ask myself, "What was it and is it like to have Dr. Larry Crabb as my father," my mind goes back to when I was about 7 years old and my brother Ken was 5. I recall Dad saying to us both, with tears in his eyes, that he would give his right arm to see us grow up to be men of God. We learned later that comment was provoked by a difficult session that involved children with some significant challenges. On June 30th, 1980, a few days after my 12th birthday, Dad started something that showed how intentional he was in raising us. At a restaurant of my choosing, after dinner he asked me a series of 11 questions that he continued to ask every year through my 21st birthday. He did the same with my brother starting on his 10th birthday. For example, he would ask questions like: *What is most important to you? What do you like most and least about yourself? What are you most afraid of? What do you think when you think about God?* As I answered each one of those 11 questions, he would write out my responses exactly as I said them. At age 13, he took me on a father-son tennis/golf extended weekend trip. During this time he gave me several letters on a variety of topics. This was also the weekend that I first began consistently beating him on the tennis court (just a quick memory).When I was 21, we went back to the same place we had gone for my 13th birthday for another father/son getaway. There he gave me a book of all my birthday (12-21) responses, with many of the letters he had written to me over the years. I sit now with this book in front of me as I reflect on the love, care, and curiosity he showed me as I grew up.

These questions have become a Crabb family tradition that he and my mother have continued with my children to this day. Once, after telling the story of my birthday dinners to a friend, I was told that I had a father who intensely loved me. My wife has often said to me, "You were raised in a fairy-tale family. And you have a mother and father who are more in love with each other now than they were on the day they married." When you talk about Larry, you have to include the love of his life since he was a 12-year-old boy, my mother Rachael. As many people know, they began dating each other at age 12 (whatever that means) and married at age 21. More than 50 years later, they are going strong with two sons and five grandchildren. Rachael has been an incredible partner to Larry. He would be quick to say that she has played the most important role in his life, aside from the Trinity, as he has pursued his calling. She was the quintessential wife and mother. She raised my brother and me as she supported Dad when he began to travel the country and world speaking. She drove us all over the Midwest as we played in tennis tournaments. It is hard to put into words what having her as my mother and Larry as my father has been like, but I can tell you how grateful, blessed, and privileged it has been to have them as my parents. The lives they have lived and continue to live, have been such an important example for everyone who knows them.

I ask again, "What has it been like to have Larry Crabb as my father?" About 5 years ago, my wife and I went through some deep waters in our relationship. Like many couples, our marriage had hit a low point, and we needed help. I asked Dad if he would be willing to spend some time with us, as we struggled with knowing what to do. For the next several months, he walked with us as we began to rebuild our relationship. To have a father who you trust and respect enough to ask to walk with you through those hard times is a rare gift. The good news is my wife and I are doing as well as we ever have – we still have ups and downs–but a renewed love and commitment for each other that Dad helped release. We are both so grateful to him for his love, time, and input.

I have a father who is not only my hero and mentor, but also my friend. As I mentioned, I am also the father of two children, Josie and Jake. As we raise these two, now young adults, I find myself leaning on my father's example and often asking for his input as we work through some of the tough decisions that many parents have to make.

Larry, now 74, has battled cancer for the past 20 years, he has remained faithful to his wife, he has poured his love into his children and grandchildren, he has helped countless people know Jesus in the midst of life's toughest moments, and he has stayed committed to putting Jesus on display by how he relates to those who know him best. To put it simply, people feel safe with him. I could easily go on with stories about Larry that show how he continues to model Christlikeness by how he lives. As he continues to wrestle with the hard questions about the "Christian life," he remains committed to "staying the course" on the narrow-road that leads to life. Someday, my heavenly Father will say to my earthly father, "Job well done my good and faithful servant!"

As Larry enters his mid-70s, I sense he is drawing close to saying what the Lord has put him here to say. He continues to follow his call as he helps guide us into the dance with the Holy Trinity. I love you Dad and cannot express how grateful I feel to be your son.

LARRY CRABB

STILL THINKING

I presume I'm qualified to offer the following opinion. Jason and Bryan have done an outstanding job of tracing the development of my thinking over the last four, nearly five decades. And the ten respondents, without exception, have each devoted considerable time to put forward thoughts about my work that I find both substantively encouraging and provocatively challenging. My sincere thanks to each of you.

In Ed Welch's response, referring to me, he wrote, "If he were not growing, he would stop writing." I have some critics who might edit Ed's words to read, "Because he is growing in the wrong direction, he ought to stop writing." I like Ed's words better. I think they are true. Much appreciated, Ed.

Growth in understanding a psychology that deserves to be called Christian requires more, but not less, than thinking with a Christian worldview always in mind;

asking hard questions answerable only through revealed truth; and, required by realistic humility, avoiding premature closure on an appealing model, never yielding to unripe certainty that breeds dogmatism. I would be remiss if I didn't mention Eric Johnson. He deserves generous credit for laying out parameters within which a truly Christian psychology must develop. Among the needed parameters, a few stand out to me as particularly important: careful biblical study to make sure our ideas about psychology either emerge from or align with Scripture; non-defensive dialogue with respected thinkers who come up with competing ideas; and respect for the findings of well-designed empirical research.

C.S. Lewis wrote of *mere* Christianity (cf. 1952/1980), the essentials of biblically informed thinking that draw the boundaries between revealed Christianity and all other world views. Only those essentials can be held with confident and comfortable certainty. Rene' Descartes, considered the father of modern philosophy, after doubting everything that could be doubted, settled his mind on his famous credo, "I think, therefore I am." In his way of thinking, perhaps that was *mere* philosophy.

I wonder how we might define *mere* Christian psychology. In my continuing desire to contribute to whatever that might be, I'm quite certain of one thing: I think, therefore I write. Doubt does a good job of plowing up hard mental soil to allow fresh thinking to grow. As I continue to exploit the opportunity of unasked for skepticism to stir further thinking, I seem to become more certain of less and less certain of more. My journey continues. Let me trace a few of its contours.

It is evident that the direction my ongoing thinking takes me is at odds with much of what is heard in today's popular Christian teaching. The message I sometimes hear from church pulpits and religious books suggests that the life we all most long for can be experienced as we travel on a road that is easier than the narrow road Jesus said is the only one that leads to life, the life made possible by His death and resurrection. I'm troubled that the psychology guiding the practice of some Christian counselors seems to regard a pleasantly healed life as a successful outcome. I worry that sincere Christ-following counselors might sometimes inadvertently lead clients on to the broad road that in the estimate of Jesus leads people to a comfortable but wasted life.

Perhaps before I die, I'll write a book titled *Confessions of a Renegade Psychologist*. I take no pleasure in oppositional thinking, opposed either to today's Americanized Christianity or secular psychology, or to some current understandings of Christian psychology, but I am concerned that a legitimately Christian interest in relieving troubling symptoms, treating underlying disorders, and promoting felt well-being could take insufficient account of what is most wrong in a fallen image bearer (and still wrong in redeemed image bearers) and what is most singularly possible only in a redeemed (though still fallen) image bearer.

To avoid that spiritual miscarriage, Christian psychology needs to be intentionally and meaningfully aware of a biblically revealed anthropology, hamartiology, and soteriology-- three fundamental theological categories. Christians who are called to wisely guide people to the healing only the Gospel offers should carefully think about what it means to bear God's relational image. They should delve into how every human being defiles his or her divine image. And they must understand some of what it means to depend on the power of God's Spirit who alone restores the image in God's people according to the Father's plan, a plan that succeeds only on the value of Christ's life, death, resurrection, and ongoing priestly work on our behalf.

Some might assume that what I'm suggesting has more to do with spiritual direction or discipleship than with counseling or therapy. My hope is to see the wisdom and purpose of spiritual direction brought into the professional work of Christian counselors.

With that hope in mind, I do my stumbling best to look at the human condition and at God's response to the mess we have made of ourselves, our relationships, and our world through the lens of God's special revelation in the Bible. Many others, of course, honor the same process and arrive at ideas different from mine. Dialogue respectful of disparate views is then called for. If I have any claim to epistemological uniqueness as I bring my thinking to the conversation, realizing that what I claim to be unique follows the lead of many thinkers before me, my claim might lie in this:

> My impetus to continue thinking and writing about the Christian life in large part comes from the exhaustion of unsatisfied desire that I endure most

days as I live in this unsatisfying world. Without the felt awareness of that exhaustion, I'm quite sure I would lose all interest in more writing.

A strange claim to epistemological uniqueness? I agree. But I find that the energy to grow in knowledge depends in significant measure on how dissatisfied I am with the impact on my life of what I believe to be true. I long to know more, and to discover the power of truth to set me free from the power of self-centeredness. Let me discuss what I mean by the phrase, "the exhaustion of unsatisfied desire."

The phrase points, I believe, to a reality in every human soul that may be partly responsible for many of the difficulties that bring people to a counselor's office. As years pass, I become more uncomfortably aware of an unquenchable thirst in a place within me deeper than my throat. It is only in brief, and sometimes sinful, seasons of nearly consuming levels of satisfaction of lesser thirsts that I am *not* conscious of a throbbing ache in my soul that presses for relief that I cannot find. C.S. Lewis warned us that an *inconsolable longing,* felt or numbed, lies in the heart of every human being, a longing more piercingly awakened in the Christian's heart.

Perhaps it was that ache which Solomon apparently experienced in the midst of enjoying every conceivable pleasure available "under the sun." He looked around and within, then concluded that "God has dealt a tragic existence to the human race" (Ecclesiastes 1:13 New Living Translation). Whatever else Solomon recognized as a tragedy in the human condition, at least two tragedies are included: (a) hunger for a full meal for the soul when only hors d'oeuvres are available and (b) thirst for ongoing gulps of living water when only irregular sips are accessible.

The tragic reality of unsatisfied desire deserves careful thought in our pursuit of a Christian psychology. Every human being, but especially Christians who all "have the first fruits of the Spirit" (Romans 8:23 English Standard Version)–which we might consider to be delicious tastes of what is to come–will live their entire lives with perhaps muted, but still powerfully alive, longings that are never fully satisfied. I think the apostle Paul would agree. In the same passage quoted above, Paul goes on to tell us that even the most spiritually mature among us will still "groan inwardly." The abundant life which Jesus made possible is abundant not always in blessings that make life into a happy experience, but rather in an abundance of the desire and ability to love well. And when our sacrificial love represents the love of Jesus, we know something of both His joy and His sorrow. Like Jesus, we groan, when we acutely and rightly desire what in His wisdom the Father does not yet make available. Joy comes as the Spirit's fruit when we delight the Father by how we love in this world and as we longingly anticipate a world made new when Jesus returns.

When we groan inwardly, only one of the two choices is then possible. On the one hand, we live to relieve or deny the existence of our inconsolable longing by whatever means we can control that seems to work, even if only for brief moments. On the other hand, we may "wait eagerly" as we live in confident hope that unmet desires in this life will forever be unfailingly and fully satisfied in the coming Eternal Day. It is that hope that frees us from demanding all the satisfaction we want now, a freedom that opens the regenerate heart to love well, like Jesus.

It's true, of course, that waiting for what God created us to enjoy tries our patience, and we cry out "How long, O Lord, how long?" The cry is legitimate. As entitled selves, however, the cry becomes a demand. Only souls surrendered to the wisdom and goodness of God's timing in the story He is telling, cry but still wait. Paul told us that surrendered souls discover God's "glorious power" as they live in a disappointing world as weary exiles, a power that enables the "endurance and patience" disciples of Christ need in order to demand nothing now (see Colossians 1:11 New Living Translation). Paul seems to connect endurance and patience with fullness of joy. That's not a connection we easily make.

As a young professional, I knew little of the exhaustion of unsatisfied desire. One of the perks of senior years is the opportunity to tremble in disappointment over unrelieved yearnings and still to trust the goodness of God. I think that brings Him more delight than thanking Him for a good life of pleasant blessings. In the days when my life was going quite well, I was only dimly aware of not having what my soul most wanted. In both my personal and professional life, my sights were not set high enough.

My training in Albert Ellis's rational-emotive therapy, now developed into cognitive-behavior therapy, seemed to line up nicely with Paul's teaching that the change made possible by the Gospel comes about through renewing our minds. His words: "let God transform you into a new person by changing the way you think" (Romans 12:2 New Living Translation). Good! I don't want to be a person moping about with unsatisfied desire. I want to see my clients enjoy their Christian life without groaning over disappointing relationships, abusive histories, and low self-esteem. If we could all trust God to operate more like a heavenly grandfather than a distant and demanding father, we could expect Him to smooth out the bumps in our lives. Think right, live well, feel good: that's the formula meant to guide the way we live and the counsel Christians offer. I would never have expressed my views in those terms, but that's how I was thinking.

Those very early days seem now to be ancient history. Had I not been challenged by mentors such as James Houston, J.I. Packer, Broughton Knox, and by mentoring authors including Jonathan Edwards, Charles Spurgeon, St. John of the Cross, and (of course) C.S. Lewis, I fear growing disillusionment with such naïve and false thinking (as described above) might have so strongly challenged my understanding of Christianity that existentialism would have become an attractive option. I knew all my training in secular psychology and my efforts to blend it with Christian thinking were not getting to the root of my clients' struggles, or mine. Christianity, as I understood it, was failing me.

As Freud once wryly commented, psychoanalysis relieves neurotic symptoms only to restore people to the misery of life. Were my therapeutic efforts doing any better? Was I merely numbing the tragedy of human existence with shallow satisfaction available to both Christians and non-Christians?

I remember being disturbed by God's indictment of spiritual leaders in Jeremiah's day: "They offer superficial treatments for my people's mortal wound" (Jeremiah 6:14 New Living Translation). Was that indictment directed to me? I longed to be a Christian counselor, not merely a counselor who happened to be a Christian, but I couldn't see how biblical truth, as I then understood it, spoke into the problems I dealt with in my professional office.

Without the abiding influence of my mentors (I didn't mention the one with the most influence, my father), disillusionment with what I thought was Christian psychology could have led me toward a strange theistic existentialism (functional deism: God exists, but He is not intimately involved in our lives. We must depend little on theology, much on psychology) or a nihilistic existentialism (outright atheism: a personal God does not exist. Best to align ourselves with whatever transcendence we can believe is real in order to find meaning, emotional stability, and personal satisfaction).

Gratefully, I acknowledge that through my mentors, the Holy Spirit drove me to take another look at the Bible, a more desperate, a more hopeful look. So many texts came alive with new life. For example, Paul warned us against teachers who deliver what "itching ears want to hear" (2 Timothy 4:4 New Living Translation). It occurred to me that the "itch" of an inconsolable longing is scratched in church and in counseling when we hear that there is a "Christian" way that we can follow to what our God-designed souls most long to experience; no need to wait till the next life for groaning to end.

Modern heirs of gnostic teaching, a teaching already alive in early form when Paul wrote to the church in Colossae, informs us that there is a secret to getting life to work as we want. There will be trouble. Christians will be assaulted with anxiety, depression, sexual addiction, feelings of inadequacy, and relational failure – the list goes on. But there is a way to move through it all to the life you most desire, a life healed of life's wounds, a much blessed life that frees you from groaning to enjoy the happiness you deserve.

Certainly as a Christian, I want to finish well. But also as a Christian psychologist, I long to more fully understand a psychology that is distinctly Christian. I do not want to re-shape biblical truth so that it scratches itching ears. The thing I most want is to never advance a "Christian" psychology that offers "a different way that pretends to be Good News but is not the Good News at all" (Galatians 1:6, 7 New Living Translation).

With sincere hope, I believe a robustly Christian psychology is well positioned to speak powerfully into life's tragic existence, into the exhaustion of unsatisfied desire, with a clear and unapologetic focus on the profound merits of Christ's death and the sustaining hope of His return, which together empowers us to walk the narrow road with no greater goal than to become spiritually formed, like Jesus.

When Christian counselors claim their advantage as Christians, their therapeutic efforts will ultimately aim toward, and never interfere with, what only resurrection power, not professional therapy and technique alone, makes possible as we live "in-between lives," in between the Cross and the Coming.

***

Enough of what is on my mind as I reflect on where my thinking is taking me. Ed was right. If I were to stop growing as a still confused, but still thinking, Christian; if I were no longer willing to wrestle with life's deepest questions whose answers prove elusive; and if I could put an end to my exhaustion with unsatisfied desire and settle for what little of God I know, I would stop writing.

After reflecting on Ed's trenchant words, I took considerable license with what he wrote and came up with what one day might serve as a fitting and telling (and, I fear, unwieldy) epitaph on my gravestone. I think the following words would mark me as a Christian psychologist whose career found its way on to the road less traveled, a mark I would gladly wear:

If he had not continued to his death trembling over (and sometimes tortured by) seasons of doubt brought on by an unsettled soul, by discomfiture with a troubling awareness of inner emptiness, and by how often God's ways both disturbed and strangely entranced him when they made no sense to his "smaller story" way of thinking; and

If by God's grace he had not remained joyfully alive with hope that God's profound love and unwavering goodness was always forming him to become, in the words of C.S. Lewis, a "little Christ", someone who could trust that a beautiful story was unfolding, a story whose outcome would provoke endless praise for the Story Teller;

Then, at some point he would have lost all interest in further efforts to write about Christian psychology and the Christian's abundant life from a decidedly evangelical perspective. He would likely have lived his final years as a burned-out cynic. But, till his death, he was still thinking.

A difficult to welcome opportunity to trust God's ways has just presented itself to me. Less than an hour ago as I was writing, a phone call informed me that yesterday a good and godly friend of more than three decades took his life. As I continue writing, after a long pause and several more phone calls, I feel hurled into dark confusion that deepens my already deep grief. I knew him well. I never suspected his occasional bouts of depression would lead him to suicide.

What was going on in his tortured soul that made ending his life on earth the chosen option? This man knew his well-studied Bible. He believed the Gospel of Christ and with fervent passion loved to let others hear the Good News. And he loved Jesus. What went wrong?

And how am I to understand God's sovereignty as I ponder this heart-breaking tragedy? Not for a moment do I believe God sovereignly caused my friend's death, but I do believe God could have met my friend with a consuming sense of His loving presence and purpose, an experience of God that would have kept him walking on his painful path. Why didn't He? I don't understand. My choice is clear. Either I give up on God or I tremble over His ways while I trust His goodness, believing He is still the Almighty God whose amazing love was revealed in Jesus.

Over the years, several times I've been brought to that choice point. An anger rises in me that makes turning my back to God seem warranted. But it's then I realize I cannot turn away from the God who died for me. I don't want to. If I were to renounce my faith in God, I would have to tell each of my mentors they were misguided fools. I could no more declare them fools than to tell the sun to never shine. When my only brother was killed in an airplane crash, my father, then the age I am now, received a one-sentence letter from his 90-year-old mentor: "You can always trust the Man who died for you". My father did. My living mentors do. My now glorified mentors still do, now without a vestige of doubt.

As I continue to write this response article, one question is now burning in my mind: What have I said in any of my books that God's Spirit could use to speak with life-sustaining power into the exhaustion of unsatisfied desire that can descend into life-denying darkness? What am I learning as I wrestle with my own messy internal world that might free me to write with more penetrating power? But I must not demand to discover a force that will do for someone what will only happen with Christ returns. I must be faithful to however God enables me to think and write, trusting Him to accomplish whatever He chooses with what He makes known to me.

In his response to Jason and Bryan's essay, my older son Kep wrote, "As Larry enters into his mid-70s, I sense he is drawing closer to saying what the Lord has put him on earth to say." The prospect enlivens me. If future books realize my son's vision, the encouragement provided to me in Jason and Bryan's article, and the thoughtful reflections offered by the ten respondents on my work so far will have played no small part in that realization.

The foundation and framework for further thinking about matters of the soul as I pursue a truly Christian understanding of psychology have been well articulated by Jason and Bryan. I thank you both for identifying the overarching themes of my work: model construction, role of the church, gender, suffering, Trinity, and new covenant theology. I'm profoundly grateful.

Two other themes continue to develop in my mind: *hamartiology,* the theology of sin. Gary Moon once told me I had done important work in developing an awareness of sin and perhaps from now on I should build on that work by emphasizing God's love for sinners. My recent book, *A Different Kind Of Happiness* (2016), focuses on the joy of loving. A second theme crystallizing in my thinking involves the value of *confusion.* As I've already mentioned, confusion requires a depth of thinking not sought after in complacency. My latest book, *When God's Ways Make No Sense* (2018), suggests that trembling in confusion can lead to trusting in mystery.

I could write many more pages if I were to relate the profitable impact of each of the respondents' thoughts. You've helped me embrace how critical it is to never present my thinking as finished, closed to competing or complementary ideas. A few words to each respondent, insufficient to express all that you've said that both encourages and challenges me, will complete my response.

Dick, you wrote "he is not done yet." Your generous support of my ideas combined with gracious scholarly concern about my teaching on gender is welcome, as is our continued friendship. Over many years, your rich scholarship has made me aware of how much I don't know, but without discouraging me from pressing on.

Ed, you commented that in *Marriage Builder* (1982), a strong belief of mine became clear: what I write must touch my soul before I present it to others. I long to honor that conviction in all I write and teach. Perhaps that is why I typically share my own struggles as backdrop to what I say.

Gary, thanks for affirming what too few appreciate: my talent as an Elvis impersonator. Even more, I was encouraged by your favorable comparison of my ideas with the thinking of our mutual friend, now with Jesus, Dallas Willard. To be compared in any way to such a brilliant and quality man is humbling. Thanks, too, for seeing me as a man with talent, moxy, and a discerning ear.

Mark, I wish I knew you better. I resonate strongly with your burden to see church community come alive with its potential to deal powerfully with troubles we too easily assume only professionals can handle. And yes, I agree there will always be a God-honoring place for traditional therapy. And yes again, grace must supply the passion for every conversation with folks struggling with failure, suffering, and relational discord, and with every other difficulty, whether in church community or a professional office.

Siang-Yang, I agree with you. Empirical research, the wisdom of church fathers and mothers, and a comprehensive assessment of major schools of psychology from a Christian world view each have their place in the work of Christian psychology. Not only do I gratefully value your faithfulness in praying for me and my family every day, I also respect your view that a rich grasp of Christian psychology requires the work of many people, each with a unique calling. I appreciate your belief that I have an important voice in developing a meaningfully *Christian* psychology.

Colin, our time together at The Cove during a School of Spiritual Direction has knit my heart with yours. Thank you for highlighting concerns about my teaching from both the right and left. Was it Churchill who said, never trust someone who has no enemies? If he is correct, I am worthy of trust. I am indebted to you for your balanced understanding of my ideas that have been challenged. One example: you explained that my focus on deep longings does not require self-obsession, but can rather lead to worship of the God who cares about them. From a distance that I regret, I highly regard what you're up to in London, and am grateful that you believe I've encouraged your good work in the church.

Bruce, it was a unique joy to hear from such an esteemed senior scholar that much of my thinking is worthy of celebration. I felt affirmed by your kindred view that "the distressing sense of God's absence and consequent loneliness creates a void in the heart which kindles desire for Him." And as you indicated, we need more Christian counselors to understand that belief in the Bible's God as a Three-Person Trinity centralizes relationship in the way we worship God and engage with others. I never want to see professional technique replace the power of relational connection in therapy. Thank you, Bruce, for taking the time to write such a thoughtful response to my work.

Jamie, to realize God used *Inside Out* (1988) to cause a paradigm shift in your theology is such a gift to me. I repeat what you reported I said to you some years ago when you told me I was a mentor to you: "I see two thirsty men meeting together for Spirit-led conversations." In your response, you spoke of the truth of the priesthood of believers, which opens the door for ordinary Christians to engage in life-changing relational encounters. We are assuredly on the same page. We truly are two thirsty men meeting to mutually profit from Spirit-led conversations.

Brett, you're correct. I am a one-prong Christian psychologist in a discipline that requires two prongs. Your comment helps me clarify my limited but, as you commented, helpful contribution to developing a

Christian psychology. The prong that I respect but have not been called to practice is scientific empirical research. Although I insist, as I believe you do, that truth clearly revealed in Scripture has authority over contrary conclusions from research, I recognize and affirm the value of research that explores much that Scripture does not clearly address. Your comment emphasizing that I teach the Christian life is not easy, and your agreement, encourages me to continue teaching what itching ears do not want to hear. It was my privilege to read a response from such a careful, honest, and gracious thinker.

Kep, words fail me. You cannot fully know what it means for a father to read such meaningful words about "what it's like to have Dr. Crabb as your father." Your journey from an active, athletic, young boy through challenging times to becoming the godly man you are today – a deeply good husband, dad, brother, son, and friend to so many – leads me to my knees in worship filled with praise, humility, wonder, and love. You once told me that I don't take myself seriously enough. That sentence came from the Spirit through your lips. From childhood, I've long been afraid that I have little to offer. Your words expressed the pride beneath my fear and began a shift to believing I have been called by God, as all Christians are, to reveal Christ to the world through whatever gifts have been given to me. I pray I will have the courage to draw even closer to saying what God has put me on earth to say. I look forward to supporting your calling to bring my legacy to many as you lead Larger Story Inc. I love you, Kep.

***

A final thought, one that follows from what I just wrote. The subtitle of Jason and Bryan's essay spoke to something deep within me: *A Career on the Road Less Traveled.* Over the years I have often worried: some people are actually listening to me. Am I leading anyone astray, away from the Good News of Jesus? That fear is still lodged somewhere in my soul. It may be a healthy fear. Conviction about what is true has a necessary place in our thinking. But dogmatism, a proud attitude that assumes one has it all together is unbecoming for anyone who stands before God. May we all move closer, perhaps slowly, never in this life to fully arrive, to an understanding of what defines Christian psychology.

References

Averbeck, R.E. (2005). The Holy Spirit in the Hebrew Bible and its connections to the New Testament. In D.B. Wallace & M.J. Sawyer (Eds.), *Who's Afraid of the Holy Spirit? An Investigation into the Ministry of the Spirit of God Today* (pp. 15-36). Dallas, Texas: Biblical Studies Press.

Averbeck, R.E. (2006). Creation and corruption, redemption and wisdom: A biblical theology foundation for counseling psychology. *Journal of Psychology and Christianity, 25,* 111-126.

Averbeck, R.E. (2008). Spirit, community, and mission: A Biblical theology for spiritual formation. *Journal of Spiritual Formation and Soul Care, 1,* 27-53.

Baxter, R. (1998). *The saints everlasting rest.* Fearn, Ros-shire, UK: Christian Heritage.

Brunner, E. (1946). *Revelation and reason.* Philadelphia, PA: Westminster.

Calvin, J. (1960). *Institutes of the Christian religion: In two volumes* (F.L. Battles, Trans.). Philadelphia: Westminster Press. (Original work published 1559)

Carter, J.D., & Narramore, B. (1979). *The integration of psychology and theology*. Grand Rapids, MI: Zondervan.

Chan, S. (1998). *Spiritual theology: A systematic study of the Christian life*. Downers Grove, IL: InterVarsity.

Collins, G.R. (1977). *The rebuilding of psychology: An integration of psychology and Christianity*. Carol Stream, IL: Tyndale House.

Crabb, L., Jr. (1971), Data and dogma as compatible. *Christianity Today, 15*(12), 539-554.

Crabb, L. Jr. (1975). *Basic principles of biblical counseling*. Grand Rapids, MI: Zondervan.

Crabb, L., Jr. (1977). *Effective biblical counseling*. Grand Rapids, MI: Zondervan.

Crabb, L., Jr. (1981). *The adventures of Captain Al Scabbard (Vols. 1-2)*. Chicago, IL: Moody.

Crabb, L., Jr. (1982/1992/2013). *The marriage builder: Creating true oneness to transform your marriage*. Grand Rapids, MI: Zondervan.

Crabb, L., Jr. (1987/2013). *Understanding people: Why we long for relationship*. Grand Rapids, MI: Zondervan.

Crabb, L., Jr. (1988/2007/2013). *Inside out.* Colorado Springs, CO: NavPress.

Crabb, L., Jr. (1991/2013). *Men and women: Enjoying the difference.* Grand Rapids, MI: Zondervan.

Crabb, L., Jr. (1993). *Finding God.* Grand Rapids, MI: Zondervan.

Crabb, L., Jr. (1995). *The silence of Adam: Becoming men of courage in a world of chaos.* Grand Rapids, MI: Zondervan.

Crabb, L., Jr. (1997). *Connecting: Healing for ourselves and our relationships.* Nashville: Thomas Nelson.

Crabb, L., Jr. (1999/2007). *The safest place on earth/Becoming a true spiritual community.* Nashville: Thomas Nelson.

Crabb, L., Jr. (2001). *Shattered dreams: God's unexpected path to joy.* Colorado Springs, CO: WaterBrook.

Crabb, L., Jr. (2002). *The pressure's off: Breaking free from rules and performance.* Colorado Springs, CO: WaterBrook.

Crabb, L., Jr. (2003). *Soul talk: The language God longs for us to speak*. Nashville: Thomas Nelson.

Crabb, L., Jr. (2006). *The PAPA prayer: The prayer you've never prayed*. Nashville: Thomas Nelson.

Crabb, L., Jr. (2009a). *66 love letters*. Nashville: Thomas Nelson.

Crabb, L., Jr. (2009b). *Real church: Does it exist? Can I find it?*. Nashville: Thomas Nelson.

Crabb, L., Jr. (2013). *Fully alive: A biblical vision of gender that frees men and women to live beyond stereotypes*. Grand Rapids, MI: Baker Books.

Crabb, L., Jr. (2015). Personal correspondence, September 17.

Crabb, L., Jr. (2016). *A different kind of happiness: Discovering the joy that comes from sacrificial love*. Grand Rapids, MI: Baker Books.

Crabb, L., Jr. (2018). *When God's ways make no sense*. Grand Rapids, MI: Baker Books.

Crabb, L., Jr., & Allender, D. (1984/2013). *Encouragement: The unexpected power of building others up*. Grand Rapids, MI: Zondervan.

Crabb, L., Jr., & Allender, D. (1985). *Hope when you're hurting*. Grand Rapids, MI: Zondervan.

Crabb, L., Jr., & Crabb, L. Sr. (1994). *God of my father: A son's reflection on his father's walk of faith*. Grand Rapids, MI: Zondervan.

Crabb, R., Reeder, S., & Calvin, D. (2015). *Listen in: Building faith and friendship through conversations that matter*. Downers Grove, IL: InterVarsity Press.

Demarest, B. (1999). *Satisfy your soul: Restoring the heart of Christian spirituality*. Colorado Springs, CO: NavPress.

Eck, B.E. (2007). Integrating the integrators: An organizing framework for a multifaceted process of integration. In D.H. Stevenson, et. al. (Eds.), *Psychology & Christianity integration: Seminal works that shaped the movement* (pp. 227-237). Batavia, IL: Christian Association for Psychological Studies.

Edwards, J. (1738/1969). *Charity and its fruits*. Edinburgh & Carlisle, PA: The Banner of Truth Trust.

Entwistle, D.N. (2015). *Integrative approaches to psychology and Christianity*. Eugene, OR: Cascade Books.

Evans, C.S. (1989). *Wisdom and humanness in psychology: Prospects for a Christian approach*. Grand Rapids, MI: Baker Book House.

Evans, C.S. (1990). *Søren Kierkegaard's Christian psychology*. Grand Rapids, MI: Baker Book House.

Freud, S. (1915/1963). The Unconscious. In *General Psychological Theory: Papers on Metapsychology* (pp. 109-146). New York: Collier Books.

Garff, J. (2007). *Søren Kierkegaard: A biography* (B.H. Kirmmse, Trans.). Princeton, NJ: Princeton University Press.

Greggo, S.P., & T.A. Sisemore. (2012). *Counseling and Christianity: Five approaches*. Downers Grove, IL: IVP Academic.

Johnson, E.L. (2007). *Foundations of soul care: A Christian psychology proposal*. Downers Grove, IL: Intervarsity Press.

Johnson, E.L. (2017). *God and soul care: The therapeutic resources of the Christian faith.* Downers Grove, IL: IVP Academic.

Johnson, E.L., & Hardin, T. (2014). Counseling and therapy from a Christian perspective [Featured Book Review of Tan, S. Y. (2011). Counseling and psychotherapy: A Christian perspective. Grand Rapids, MI: Baker Academic]. *Journal of Psychology and Theology, 42,* 382-385.

Johnson, E.L., & Myers, D.G. (2010). *Psychology and Christianity: Five views.* Downers Grove, IL: IVP Academic.

Jones E. (1953-57). *The life and work of Sigmund Freud.* New York: Basic Books.

Jones, S. & Butman, R.E. (2011). *Modern psychotherapies: A comprehensive Christian appraisal.* (2nd Edition). Downers Grove, IL: IVP Academic.

Joubert, N. (2018). *Psychology and psychotherapy in the perspective of Christian anthropology.* Newcastle upon Tyne, UK: Cambridge Scholars Publishing.

Kierkegaard, S. (1980). *The sickness unto death.* (H.V. Hong & E.H. Hong, Eds. and Trans.). Princeton, NJ: Princeton University Press.

Knabb, J.J. (2016). *Faith-based ACT for Christian clients: An integrative treatment approach.* New York, NY: Routledge.

Knabb, J.J. (2017). *Acceptance and commitment therapy for Christian clients: A faith-based workbook.* New York, NY: Routledge.

Knabb, J.J., & Frederick, T.V. (2017). *Contemplative prayer for Christians with chronic worry: An eight-week program.* New York, NY: Routledge.

Knabb, J.J., Frederick, T.V., & Cumming III, G. (2017). Surrendering to God's providence: A three-part study on providence-focused therapy for recurrent worry (PFT-RW). *Psychology of Religion and Spirituality, 9,* 180-196.

Lambert. H. (2011). *The biblical counseling movement after Adams.* Wheaton, IL: Crossway.

Lewis, C.S., (1949). *The Weight of Glory.* New York: The Macmillan Company.

Lewis, C.S. (2007). *The Collected Letters of C.S. Lewis, Vol. III, Narnia, Cambridge and Joy, 1950-1963.* W. Hooper (Ed.). San Francisco: Harper.

Lewis, C.S. (1972). *God in the dock: Essays on theology and ethics.* Grand Rapids, MI: Eerdmans.

May, W. (Ed.). (2012-2019). *Christian psychology around the world*. Retrieved from https://emcapp.ignis.de/.

Merton, T. (1979). *Seeds of contemplation*. Westport, CT: Greenwood.

Mother Teresa. (2007). *Mother Teresa: Come be my light: The private writings of the "Saint of Calcutta"*. B. Kolodiejchuk (Ed.), New York, NY: Doubleday.

Oden, T.C. (1984). *Care of souls in the classic tradition*. Philadelphia, PA: Fortress Press.

Oden, T.C. (1992). The historic pastoral care tradition: A resource for Christian psychologists. *Journal of Psychology and Theology, 20*, 137-146.

Pennington, M.B. (1980). *Centering prayer*. New York, NY: Doubleday.

Peterson, E. (2005). *Christ plays in a thousand places: A conversation in spiritual theology*. Grand Rapids: Eerdmans.

Piper, J. (1986). *Desiring God: Meditations of a Christian hedonist*. Portland, OR: Multnomah.

Roberts, R.C. (1988). Therapies and the grammar of a virtue. In R.H. Bell (Ed.), *The grammar of the heart: New essays in moral philosophy & theology* (pp. 149-170). San Francisco: Harper & Row.

Rosales, A., & Tan, S.Y. (2016). Acceptance and commitment therapy (ACT): Empirical evidence and clinical applications from a Christian perspective. *Journal of Psychology and Christianity, 35*, 269-275.

Smith, C. (2003). Introduction: Rethinking the secularization of American public life. In C. Smith (Ed.), *The secular revolution: Power, interests, and conflict in the secularization of American public life* (pp. 1-96). Berkeley, CA: University of California Press.

Tan, S.Y. (2011a). *Counseling and psychotherapy: A Christian perspective.* Grand Rapids, MI: Baker Academic.

Tan, S.Y. (2011b). Mindfulness and acceptance-based cognitive behavioral therapies: Empirical evidence and clinical applications from a Christian perspective. *Journal of Psychology and Christianity, 30*, 243-249.

Tan, S. Y., & Scalise, E. (2016). *Lay counseling: Equipping Christians for a helping ministry* (2nd ed.), Grand Rapids, MI: Zondervan.

Teresa of Avila (1979). *The interior castle*. New York, NY: Paulist.

Welch, E.T. (1994). Who are we? Needs, longings, and the image of God in man. *Journal of Biblical Counseling, 13*(1), 25-38.

Willard, D. (1988). *The spirit of the disciplines*. San Francisco: Harper.

Willard, D. (1997). *The divine conspiracy: Rediscovering our hidden life in God*. San Francisco: Harper.

Willard, D. (2002). *Renovation of the heart: Putting on the character of Christ*. Colorado Springs: NavPress.

Willard, D. (2009). *Knowing Christ today: Why we can trust spiritual knowledge*. New York: HarperCollins.

Willard, D. (1984/2012). *Hearing God: Developing a conversational relationship with God*. Downers Grove, IL. IVP Books.

Worthington, E.L., Jr., Johnson, E.L., Hook, J.N., & Aten, J.D. (Eds.). (2013). *Evidence-based practices for Christian counseling and psychotherapy*. Downers Grove, IL: IVP Academic.

For more information about Dr. Larry Crabb:

Dr. Crabb founded *NewWay Ministries©* in 2002 to "ignite a revolution in relationships" through conference teachings, schools for spiritual direction, and writing. You can learn more about NewWay Ministries at www.newministries.org.

Larger Story© was launched in 2019 by Dr. Crabb's son, Kep, as a legacy project to continue the work his father had started, bringing together the books, sermons, talks, and videos spanning his prolific career. Learn more about Larger Story at largerstory.com

For more information about the Gideon Institute:

HBU | THE GIDEON INSTITUTE
COUNSELING CENTER

The *Gideon Institute for Christian Psychology and Counseling* at Houston Baptist University was started in 2019 to "foster Christ-centered, biblically rooted, and scientifically informed psychology and soul care." You can learn more at https://hbu.edu/college-of-education-and-behavioral-sciences/gideon-institute/

Made in the USA
Monee, IL
27 February 2020

22355019R00098